T0288392

BAY BOY

BAY BOY

STORIES OF A CHILDHOOD
IN POINT CLEAR, ALABAMA

WATT KEY

ILLUSTRATIONS BY MURRAY KEY

FOREWORD BY JOHN S. SLEDGE

The University of Alabama Press   Tuscaloosa

The University of Alabama Press
Tuscaloosa, Alabama 35487-0380
uapress.ua.edu

Inquiries about reproducing material from this work
should be addressed to the University of Alabama Press.

Typeface: Scala Pro

Cover art: Murray Key
Cover design: Michele Myatt Quinn

Cataloging-in-Publication data is available from
the Library of Congress.
ISBN: 978-0-8173-2035-5
E-ISBN: 978-0-8173-9263-5

For Mom and Dad. Good job.

CONTENTS

CONTENTS

FOREWORD BY JOHN S. SLEDGE

MOBILE BAY HAS BEEN A boy's paradise since long before the Spaniards first charted its waters five centuries ago. Its brown sandy beaches, gently shelving floor, balmy summer temperatures, and marine abundance have always beckoned adventurous spirits. During the 1970s and '80s, when many American kids were perched in front of the boob tube mesmerized by *The Brady Bunch*, *Happy Days*, and *Welcome Back, Kotter*, Albert Watkins Key Jr., familiarly known as "Watt," was growing up in an uninsulated scantling-board summer house at Point Clear, midway down the bay's Eastern Shore, sucking the very marrow of life from the surrounding woodlands and waters. His genius, and our good fortune, is that he has spun those experiences into such an engaging series of essays, collected here for the first time.

Key's Point Clear was not the tony enclave of today with its spas, designer jewelry, and two-million-dollar waterfront lots. Rather, it was a sleepy resort community, practically deserted in the winter, so quiet that (as Watt says in this book), one could hear "a screen door slam for a quarter mile" and "the thrumming of diesel engines in the ship channel." Key admits that even his own three children sometimes have trouble fathoming their father's childhood. They cannot imagine his preference for swimming in the bay rather than the Grand Hotel's enormous pool—there are stingrays and the water "makes your underwear brown"—nor how he and his six younger siblings endured having no air-conditioning—"we spent almost every night of the summer on army cots on the wharf." Mercifully spared television and video games, Key filled his hours collecting driftwood to make forts, scooting around the bay in a sturdy Stauter-Built boat, and doing art and writing stories when it rained.

There is no literary artifice in these pages. Key has made his reputation as a young-adult novelist, and appropriately his tone here is simple and direct, punctuated by laugh-out-loud moments. His parents are mostly off-page, but when they do appear, they display an old-school style of wise semidetachment that is positively refreshing in this era of helicopter parents. For example, at sixteen years of age, "sick of chores" and "sick of curfews," Key announces his decision to run away and live in the woods. Rather than argue with him, his mother's disarming response is, "Well, that sure does sound like fun." She wishes him well and lets him go. He returns after one night, angst relieved.

Other adventures are genuinely dangerous, none more so than when Key and two brothers illegally spend the night inside Middle Bay Lighthouse, an 1885 hexagonal screw-pile structure standing in eleven feet of water more than two miles offshore. They arrive and clamber up the ladder, anchoring their Boston Whaler well away from the pilings. Thunder awakens them the next morning, and they behold "Mobile Bay whipped into six-foot seas." Incredibly, the boys risk swimming for their boat, fearful lest it drift off and strand them. Many a more experienced and careful hand than young Watt Key has lost his life in Mobile Bay in similar circumstances, but fortunately the aspiring writer survived to relate this episode like the good sea story that it is.

Just like Watt's first essay collection, 2015's *Among the Swamp People, Bay Boy* includes some colorful characters—Mad Bill Dickson, a curmudgeonly tow truck driver; I'llNeeda, a middle-aged homeless woman encamped in a shack across the road; and the Ghost of Zundel's Wharf, "the restless soul of a long-dead construction worker." But it is the youthful Key himself who is to the fore in these pieces, and the effect is altogether salutatory. Whereas his first collection focused on his adult years exploring the delta, this one highlights a happy coastal boyhood. Everything one would expect to be covered in such a book is here, including Mardi Gras, shrimping, fishing, dove hunting, hurricanes, jubilees, and camping out, to name but a few.

It is pleasant to think of *Bay Boy* gracing the coffee tables of cottages and condominiums along Alabama's shores. But it is even more satisfying to think of it in homes far from lapping waves, salt breezes, and swaying moss. Mobile Bay is famous in song and story, and Watt Key now joins the distinguished ranks of those writers who have helped make it so. If, after half an hour absorbed in these pages, you do not immediately make travel plans to gaze upon these lovely tawny waters for yourself, I for one shall be surprised.

INTRODUCTION BY THE AUTHOR

OFFICIALLY I'M A NATIVE OF Tuscaloosa, Alabama, but it's hard to think of myself that way. My parents had me, the first of seven children, while my father was still in school at the University of Alabama. Upon his graduation, they moved into my grandfather's vacation home in Point Clear, where my father had summered as a boy. I was two years old then, and it's the only childhood home I can remember.

Point Clear has long been famous as a resort area and retirement community for the wealthy. But it is also a place where locals, like me, lived, worked, and played. This collection showcases a special place from the perspective of a young boy in the '70s and '80s. Some of them are funny, some are sad, and some are historical essays. All of them are meant to be shared and read aloud by all ages.

Our house was called Little Fish, after my grandmother whose first name was Fisher. It was designed as a summer cottage, not for year-round living, much less for a family of nine. But life in Point Clear is really about being outside anyway. I have never found a place so perfectly suited to exercise a young boy's imagination. Fifty feet from our front door were the brackish waters of Mobile Bay, teeming with speckled trout, redfish, flounder, and blue crabs. Out our back door was Caldwell Swamp, a mysterious bog of bay trees, magnolia, and slash pine. Thirty miles south of us were the jade green waters of the Gulf of

Mexico, and half that distance to the north was the second largest river delta in the country. It is a place where one can't help feeling the wonders and beauty of nature. It's a place where a young writer can wonder a lot and want to write about it.

Most of the stories contained in this collection were originally published by *Mobile Bay* magazine. They are all true, or told to me as truth. Some names have been changed for obvious and not so obvious reasons.

THE NEW OLD POINT CLEAR

I SUDDENLY FIND MYSELF AT the age where I'm telling my kids "how it used to be when I was growing up." I remember when my father and grandfather told me these same kinds of stories. And they successfully convinced me that life in Point Clear, Alabama, was more interesting back in their day. It's certainly true that my six siblings and I grew up with paved roads and we didn't have to ride a ferry to get into the city. But, with hindsight, it seems every generation has some interesting stories to pass down.

Scenic Highway 98 was asphalted by the time I was born in 1970, but there still weren't many people living in Point Clear year-round.

"It used to be a dirt road!" one of my kids exclaimed.

"That's right," I said. "When your great-grandfather built this house."

"Of course, the summers were still full of vacationers, and having grown up across the bay in Mobile, your grandmother knew most of them. Since we were always around, her friends would bring their kids by. Between me and all your aunts and uncles, there was always somebody the right age to play with. And there was plenty to do."

"Like what?" my son asks.

"We'd swim in the bay and fish and build forts and rope swings. Ride in the boat. You know that little wooden boat I fixed up for you? That used to be mine. It had an old motor that would run most of the time. But sometimes we'd break down or run out of gas."

"You broke down out there?"

"Sometimes. Part of the fun was getting home. It's shallow enough to walk your boat in from just about anywhere."

"But you didn't have video games, right, Dad?"

"No, we didn't have video games."

"Man," my son says.

"Did you have a pool?" my daughter asks.

"The Grand Hotel had a pool, and we'd go up there sometimes, but we mostly swam in the bay."

"But it makes your underwear brown," my son says. "And there's stingrays."

"We had a lot of brown underwear, but I never knew anyone that was stuck by a stingray."

"Where would everybody sleep?"

"We didn't have air-conditioning so we spent almost every night of the summer on army cots on the wharf."

"Like camping?"

"Yes. It was cooler out there."

"What about mosquitoes?"

"You'd have to get under a sheet if there wasn't a breeze to keep them away. Every now and then our friends got scared and we'd come inside."

"And it was really hot?"

"Sometimes. The boys' room was at the back of the house near the highway. There was never a breeze back there. The little kids slept naked on the carpet under a ceiling fan."

"Dad!"

"The big ones slept beside them in their bathing suits."

"Didn't y'all have beds?"

"Sure, we had beds, but it was cooler on the floor."

"What about when summer was over?"

"People rolled canvas down over their screen porches, they hauled their boats out of the water, and everyone went back to the city. It felt like a big party was ending. Then the blustery southwest wind turned into a cool eastern breeze and the bay got real calm. By Halloween it was so quiet that you could hear a screen door slam for a quarter mile. Sometimes a lonely dog barked at night. Ships moaned out in the channel. There was so little traffic on the road that I remember nights lying on my back in the middle of the blacktop, feeling the warm rocks through my shirt. If a car was out, I heard it from a mile away like a train coming down the tracks."

"Like Indians," my son says.

"Yeah . . . But don't do that . . . And don't tell your mother I told you that. The road's a lot more dangerous now than it used to be."

My kids grow silent for a moment.

"Didn't you get bored?" my daughter asks.

"Your grandmother always said, 'Only boring people get bored.' Even when the cold north wind came in winter and rattled the front windows and the bay was rough and brown like chocolate milk, we had plenty to do. We had the big swamp across the road, where we built forts out of driftwood. And when it was rainy outside, we'd draw and make things. I'd write stories."

"You never watched television?"

"Sometimes on Sunday nights we did. But we only had three channels and it was black-and-white."

"What's that?"

"It wasn't in color."

"Was the house real cold, Dad?"

"It was so cold that we had to get dressed in front of a gas heater. We got so close to the flames that the house smelled like burnt hair in the mornings."

My daughter's face drooped into sadness. "Sounds like y'all were real poor."

"No, the house just wasn't meant to be a year-round house. And not everybody had central heat and air-conditioning like we have now."

"But one time you told us Aunt Alice sold your toys."

"Well, yes, but she sold them to *us*. There were so many kids in our house that she could set up a table just outside the kitchen and sell things to the rest of the family. It was mostly all of our toys that we'd left out. And sometimes, if you bought something from her and left it out again, she'd hide it away. Then you'd have to buy it back from her the next time she opened her store."

"But it was already *yours*."

"It got confusing."

"I'm glad I didn't live in the old days," my daughter says.

"But there's lots of good stories," my son says. "Tell us about the time you spent the night in Middle Bay Lighthouse and the big storm came."

"And the time you had to raise all the wild pigs in the yard."

"And the time you ran away from home and lived on the river."

"I don't know if we have time for all that tonight. But I'll tell you what. Y'all get some sleep and I'll tell you some more tomorrow."

GOVERNMENT HOUSING

ALL OLD HOUSES HAVE GOOD stories to tell. Our house on the bay is no exception. It was paid for by the US government.

My grandfather was from Marshall, Texas. He didn't discover Alabama until he joined the Navy and was stationed in Mobile as a naval engineer during the Second World War. As the war dragged on, he and my grandmother decided to look for a quieter place to rent outside the city. They subsequently discovered Point Clear.

When the war was over, my grandfather moved back to Texas, but Point Clear stayed on his mind. He wanted to build a second home there one day, but at the time, everyone was focused more on rebuilding their lives than on planning vacation homes.

Back in Texas, my grandfather and his two brothers formed a company called Key & Key Brothers. Like most people after the war, they were trying to figure out how to make a living. At the time, the government ran enormous auctions to dispose of military surplus. Deciding to focus on this opportunity, the brothers purchased a warehouse in Jefferson. They used some of the space for their offices and the rest for stocking an inventory of surplus hardware.

Seeing an advertisement for "computers," my grandfather entered a bid of slightly less than five cents each for what he assumed were slide rules, manual plastic ruler-like devices common in that day. These instruments typically sold for nearly one dollar and he anticipated an easy profit.

It wasn't long before the government agent contacted them with news that they'd won the bid, and 168 computers were at a storage facility in San Antonio, ready for pickup. San Antonio was several hours away by car, a trip that would substantially cut into their profit margins.

"Can you ship them to us?" my grandfather asked.

The agent said this wasn't possible.

"We'll pay the postage."

"It's going to take more than a little postage to get these things out of here," the agent replied. "A parallax computer in its crate is a 270-pound electronic fire control instrument. The 168 computers are taking up nearly an acre of our facility."

My grandfather explained there had been a misunderstanding but the agent wasn't sympathetic. He insisted that a deal had been made and that Key & Key Brothers was contractually obligated to have the merchandise removed from the premises.

The Key brothers reluctantly shelled out $4,000 to have their $6.89 purchase shipped to Jefferson and stored in their warehouse. Then they dusted their hands of the disaster and focused once again on other, more profitable merchandise.

Several years later, just before the start of the Korean War, a procurement officer from the Air Force walked into the warehouse of Key & Key Brothers. He explained he'd been sent to inquire about classified military technology that had been mistakenly auctioned to their firm. After the agent described the items, my grandfather recalled the old computers.

"We still have them," he said. "Stacked against the back wall of the building. Not even opened."

The agent then agreed to pay $63,000 for the merchandise, which would have cost them $1,000,000 if ordered new from the manufacturer.

As it turned out, these computers were considered to be one of the greatest technological innovations to come out of the Second World War, so highly classified that their operators were instructed to sacrifice their lives before revealing them to the enemy. They were used in B-29 bombers to operate the Central Station Fire Control System (CSFC). Prior to the CSFC, each turret in a bomber required a gunner to manually aim the weapons. The CSFC used the plane's altitude, airspeed, and temperature to calculate the proper aiming of the guns so that they could be fired remotely from a centralized location in the plane. These same devices had been used to drop the atomic bombs on Japan.

The Key brothers accepted what they considered a very generous offer. Subsequently, the November 20, 1950, issue of *Time* magazine ran an article called "The Country Boy," in which they recounted the story of my grandfather (the "Country Boy") and the parallax computer debacle. Then Texas Senator Lyndon Johnson called it "the most astounding case of shortsightedness that we have ever encountered."

With his share of the proceeds, my grandfather purchased a lot in Point Clear and built his vacation home. A home he would later pass to my father, and where I was raised. Until Hurricane Katrina, the fence pickets around the house were made from the packing crates of the parallax computers.

ARTS AND CRAFTS IN POINT CLEAR

WE DIDN'T HAVE VIDEO GAMES and we didn't watch much television. I recall watching episodes of *Little House on the Prairie* on Sunday nights. Mom and Aunt Ella sewed and watched soap operas together while we were at school. I remember the music from *The Guiding Light* drifting through the house whenever I was sick and stayed home. To this day that music makes me queasy.

From an early age, Mom enforced outside play and making things in lieu of television. I'm sure she was eager to get seven kids out of the house, but she also has a knack for crafts and likes to see people "doing something." And if you ever needed a suggestion about *what* to do, she was full of ideas.

A favorite of ours was the art sale. Those of us who were more creatively inclined enjoyed the art aspect of it. The rest of the siblings put forth their best effort in anticipation of the profits.

Mom provided a large roll of newsprint for us to tear away pieces to use as a canvas. Then she brought out crayons, finger paint, glitter, pipe cleaners, yarn, and other miscellaneous items to decorate with. After we spent a couple of hours building an inventory of artwork, it was time for the sale. Mom stretched a clothesline out near the highway and we hung our pictures with clothespins like laundry. Then we sat in the driveway and waited for customers.

And waited . . .

In winter, the art sale business was slow. We got, perhaps, a passing car every ten minutes. And the only people who ever stopped were my grandparents and Aunt Ella. Somehow, they always seemed to be driving by when we had art sales. Summer was more exciting. With our cousins over from Mobile, business nearly doubled. Regardless, we always had at least two customers and we were sure to sell out our inventory and walk away with about seventy-five cents in our pockets.

Once I outgrew art sales, I preferred spending my free time on the bay or in the woods. When it came to crafts, I was into making things out of animal hides from various critters I hunted and trapped. One day I shot a squirrel in the backyard, skinned it, nailed its hide to a board, and poured Morton Salt over it. I let it sit for a couple of weeks until the smell was tolerable. When I finally took it off the board, it was stiff as a shoe sole. I'd heard Indians chewed on hides to make them soft, but I wasn't ready for that, and the project was already taking too long. I folded the hide in half, stapled the edges, added a red yarn shoulder strap, and presented the purse to Mom on Easter morning. Tail on. She took it to mass.

The girls moved on to making pot holders. Then they graduated to beading and jewelry. My young brothers turned to making weapons. They created slingshots, blowguns, clubs, spears, and other devices that didn't fit a category. The most terrifying of these was the cheese grater on a broomstick. It was acceptable for even the oldest brother (me) to run for his life when someone brandished the cheese grater stick.

Trips to Fairhope Hardware were few and far between. We had to thoroughly scavenge the house, the beach, and the yard for supplies. Occasionally my parents missed things that found their way into someone's creation. Dad's valuable hand-painted lead soldiers, which he'd played with as a boy, were smelted into a baseball-size mace. The tail feathers were plucked from Mom's live rooster to complete an Indian headdress. Her new sheets were confiscated for the sail of a raft.

I was gone to college by the time my brothers progressed to more complicated weapons such as bows and arrows, atlatls, and battle-axes. Then they outgrew the arena of our backyard and took their act on the road.

When I was home one weekend, Murray asked me to drive him and our youngest brother, David, to the Battle of Fort Mims reenactment. They were going to take their homemade weapons and play Indians in the show. Murray had done it before, but it was eight year-old David's first public appearance.

When I parked the car next to a field crowded with spectators, I assumed David was getting dressed in the back seat. But I was shocked to see him jump out of the car and run across the battlefield, seemingly naked. Then I saw the string from his loincloth tracing just above his bare buttocks.

"Can he wear that?" I asked Murray.

"Yeah," Murray said. "He's an Indian."

Some of the siblings exercised their artistic license to a greater extent than the rest of us.

These days my creative efforts are mainly focused on writing, but I still check myself if I wind up in front of a television for too long. One afternoon I was driving through the countryside and passed a yard full of scrap iron creations. Out front was a sign that said:

LOOK WHAT I DID WHILE YOU WERE WATCHING TV

I like that person's attitude.

THE LONGEST DAY OF THE YEAR

BY THE TIME CHRISTMAS ARRIVED in Point Clear, the bay was too cold and rough and shallow to enjoy. The wharf house existed like a summer cottage we'd left boarded up for the winter, except we could still see it through the front window, way out there through the north wind and the wet and the spray. Occasionally I'd have to run out to fasten a slamming door or secure something, and it was always weird and lonely.

On Christmas Eve, Dad built a fire in the fireplace and we sat around as he read *The Night before Christmas*. The men in our family have always been good storytellers, but I don't ever recall this tale being much of a thriller. I think it was just a visual for Mom's benefit.

After the story, we wrote wish lists on tissue paper and tossed them into the fire. The objective was for the draft to take the letters up the chimney to Santa, but we saw some of them burn up. Which was fine. According to Mom, Santa could read smoke, too. We weren't really concerned until Dad forgot to get up early one morning and pick the unburned ones off the lawn.

After a long night of much wide-eyed boredom, Mom came to release us at daybreak. We scampered into the living room and plunged into our separate piles of gifts. Santa was always good to us, and until about eight thirty, we were blissfully forgetful of the impending doom.

"Time to get ready for church," Mom eventually announced.

Those words hit me in the gut. It was time to get cinched into Sunday clothes and make our annual trip to Mobile.

When I was a child, the journey across the bay brought to mind uncomfortable clothes, boring church, old people, and carsickness.

We piled into the green station wagon, itching in our Sunday outfits and irritable at having to leave our new gifts idle on the living room floor for the rest of the day. We made the long trip up the Eastern Shore, across the causeway, and through the tunnel into the city.

First stop was the Cathedral Basilica. We were always late and caused considerable commotion as our family of nine entered the cavernous, echoing building. We sat at the rear of the church with most of the siblings in the back row and Mom, Dad, and the babies in the row in front of us. A cathedral mass was more serious and boring than our usual church. The only practical way to pass time was to see how often you could get away with going to the bathroom. But the back bathroom under the staircase was creepy like maybe a hunchback was lurking in the shadows. I didn't ever want to stay long. Dad really had it the best. Typically he wasn't one to cuddle babies, but he loved babies in church. And as soon as they would so much as peep, he was out the back door with it.

One year a brother positioned himself on the outside near the aisle. As the priest delivered mass, the rest of us children shifted and twitched and stood and knelt and giggled and elbowed and shushed. All the while we suspected the brother on the end was actually being good. He was still and quiet and keeping his hands to himself. Actually, he was using his fingers to slowly work at the nut on a bolt beneath his left leg. Suddenly there was a giant crack and the upright supporting the pew slammed out into the marble floor and the bench collapsed and we all slid into the aisle.

If you dropped a dime at the back of the cathedral, it would probably turn heads halfway to the altar. Dropping a church pew halts mass.

The priest stopped talking while we scrambled to our feet and started trying to put it all together again. I still think it was strange that nobody offered to help. They just turned and stared like it was something they were watching on television. Then I felt Dad tap my arm.

"I think it's just time to go, son," he said.

After the cathedral we went to my great-grandmother's house on West Street for lunch with more cousins. We called her Nannie, and she was ninety-something years old for most of my life. She was the most ancient living person I knew, a mummy unwrapped, a skeleton with lipstick. But old as she was, her mind was sharp. She remembered all of our names, something that most of my Mobile cousins couldn't achieve. And she was ultimately responsible for me getting to know my extended family in the big city.

But to us kids, Nannie's lunch was just one more thing keeping us from our gifts at home. And her old house was stuffy and packed with more old people. We eventually found our way onto the porch and into the yard to get air and relief with the rest of our young cousins. By one o'clock we were lying on the lawn, our Sunday clothes already dirty and starting to come off. Waiting for our parents to stop talking and come on. But there was only more misery to come. A long day of being carted around Mobile, seeing my mother's friends, watching their children play with their new toys, thinking about our new toys way over across the bay. We just wanted to go home.

We got back to Point Clear late in the afternoon, puddled in the back of the green station wagon, tired, carsick, our Sunday clothes unbuttoned and dirty. I remember just wanting some air. It was the one day of winter I wanted to walk out on the windblown wharf and sit there.

THE GREEN STATION WAGON

WHEN I THINK OF THE depths of winter, I recall sounds. Many nights I lay in my bed, listening. The north wind rattled the windows when a cold front blew through. The gas heaters in the house ticked and popped against it. The next morning found a crisp silence left in its wake. Overlaying that silence was the thrumming of diesel engines in the ship channel, the croaking of blue herons, and the occasional yawing of a chainsaw. And late that night, always after a cold front for some reason, came the street racers.

We lived along the middle of a straightaway on Scenic Highway 98. My bedroom was closest to the road. In the late-night hours this remote stretch of blacktop was often used for clandestine street racing. I listened to them coming from a half-mile away, roaring past at what was surely over a hundred miles per hour.

I always wondered what these cars looked like, where they came from, and who drove them. I had my suspicions. There was Creech's Repair Shop up County Road 32. It was nothing more than a couple of barns and a grassy lot. Some kind of race boat or race car project was always going on there. And my school bus passed several other yards where skinny, hungry-looking, coyote-faced people worked on hot rods under shade trees. To this day, those night races remain a mystery to me.

Our own cars over the years were impressive, but in a different way.

The green station wagon is the first I remember well. Dad bought it used from the Red Cross auction, but we considered it new. The car really had two distinct eras—before the pine tree and after the pine tree.

Before the pine tree, the green station wagon took us on two family trips per year: Disney World in spring and West Texas in summer. There were no seat belt laws back then, so it was like a portable corral for all of us kids. Mom bought a sack full of cheap toys at TG&Y and dumped them in the back like chicken feed, and Dad hit the interstate.

The air-conditioning didn't work well so we rode with the windows down much of the time. Of course, if it rained, we rolled them up. But the biggest threat from rain was not spray coming in the window, it was "the hole."

It didn't take long for us to wear through the carpet. In the second row of seats—on the floor behind the passenger's side, a metal plate about the size of a hockey puck was revealed. I still don't know why it was there, almost like a drain for the car if it were to flood. For a while the plate was sealed to the floor with something like tar. It didn't take us long to pick the black glue away and pry it off. The hole literally opened a world of opportunity.

We soon found that hitting a puddle at anything over twenty miles per hour created a muddy geyser that pounded the ceiling like it was going to buckle metal. Dad was typically on edge while driving us about town and this never failed to push him over the precipice.

"Somebody put their foot back over the damn hole!"

But that was just on rainy days. On any other day, the hole was as useful as if it had been planned.

Service station attendants never ceased to be amazed at the little mound of trash that suddenly appeared from beneath our car when it pulled away from the gas pumps. And when we were under way, all operations at the hole were hidden from our parents' view. Don't want the rest of what you're eating? No problem. Can't finish your drink? No problem. Need to pee and Dad won't pull over? No problem.

Outside of the geysers, the hole never caused any problems until I decided to drop a Grand Hotel golf ball out of it on the way to church. The ball bounced between the highway and the gas tank with such violence that it sounded like a machine gun was going off in the car. Mom swerved across the road a few times, trying to dodge and shake it, and finally veered into the ditch. Once the station wagon was stopped, she turned in her seat with a "What the hell happened!" look.

"That was cool," one of my younger brothers said.

Hurricane Frederic marked the beginning of the "after the pine tree" years. The green station wagon was crushed long-ways beneath an enormous pine tree. Even though Dad intended to salvage it, he decided Mom needed a new vehicle. They'd seen something called a Chevrolet Suburban on the last trip to Texas and it seemed just the thing for our ever-growing family.

Mom got the Suburban and Dad used a car jack to bend the ceiling back up in the green station wagon. After he replaced the glass, we had our new hunting vehicle.

It wasn't perfect. The left passenger-side door wouldn't latch, so he had a rope that tied it closed. The luggage rack banged against the roof if you went over fifty miles per hour, and the windshield wipers flew off on the highest setting. But we still had the hole. And to me, as long as we had the hole, the green station wagon was still as good as new.

PETS

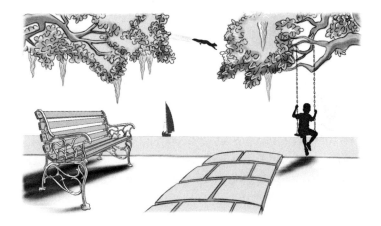

LATE WINTER ON THE BAY is wet and windy and cold. I recall staring out the front windows, watching waves crash against the bulkhead and raindrops roll down the glass. The Christmas tree was long gone from its place in the corner. Hunting season was over. There was a lot of nasty weather left before spring and a lot of school left before summer. Life in Point Clear is all about waiting for summer.

Even in my adult life, February and early March are wet spots in my head that I have to slog through. When I was a child, this time of year was when we were most alone. And when I try to remember what I did with my time, I recall waiting for the rain to stop and finally going outside under gray skies and dripping pine needles and sidestepping magnolia leaves cupped with water. There doesn't seem to be any smell to February, as if the rains wash it out. And it's quiet, and no matter how you dress, the cold of it licks your bones.

Around our house you never wanted to advertise you were bored. That was as good as asking for a job. It was better for all involved if you disappeared and got over it. So I crossed the highway to the small lot where we had a dog yard, a chicken coop, rabbit cages, and a barn for storing boats and old cars and clutter. I spent a lot of my childhood around the barn as I was responsible for tending the animals that lived over there.

Aside from your typical dogs and cats and rabbits, we had more unusual creatures that created unusual challenges.

While chickens weren't the most exotic, they took up most of my time and resentment. Our rooster, Leghorn, was crazy. He didn't just crow in the mornings, but all day long and into the night like an insane prisoner. I had to get past him every day to check for chicken eggs. One step into his coop and it was likely he'd be on you like a convict with feet full of knives.

Leghorn was the scariest, but Sally the possum was by far the meanest, evilest creature I'd ever brought back from the woods. I caught her in a plywood box trap I'd hammered together and decided it would be interesting to train a possum.

I transferred Sally to the rabbit cages and tried to befriend her. But no one could get within two feet of the wire mesh before she tensed up and opened her mouth in that slow way possums will do, baring a nightmarish set of teeth and hissing like she could move a lot faster if given the opportunity. I tried feeding her everything from lettuce to toads, but she wouldn't take any of it.

I finally decided Sally was too stubborn for training and should go back to the woods, but she couldn't free herself and I was too scared to release her. After trying many extraction techniques, I eventually kicked the rabbit cage off its stand, flipped the door open with a broomstick, and ran. Sally waddled away, no faster than ever.

The prize for most chaotic pets goes to the wild pigs. I shot their mother at the hunting camp and felt guilty when I approached her and found she had piglets. I collected all six of them and brought them home. From clear across the highway, I heard them squealing and grunting and rooting up the dog yard. I was amazed at how fast they grew and how much they ate. It wasn't long before I felt I'd done my penance and we hauled them to a local farmer.

Of all my strange pets, Smokey the gray squirrel was my favorite. One blustery March afternoon my next-door neighbor walked over and told me that he'd found three baby gray squirrels blown from their nest. One of them was already dead but the other two were still alive. He said I could have them if I wanted.

The squirrels were pink and hairless and fit side by side in the palm of my hand. They'd suffered exposure and ant bites and Mom told me it wasn't likely they'd live. She got down the chicken egg incubator, put some dishrags in the bottom, and plugged it up on the kitchen counter.

One of the squirrels died within the first day but the last one continued to hold on. After a few more days he was taking milk from the rabbit bottle and squirming about. A soft layer of smoke gray hair began to appear on him and I called him Smokey.

Smokey stayed in the incubator, wrapped in warm blankets, until he opened his eyes a couple of weeks later. Once he was strong enough, he found a home in a cardboard box in my bedroom. Soon he accompanied me about the house, clutching my shirt or locked on to the top of my head like a toupee with a face and tail.

It wasn't long before Smokey was able to get out of his box and explore the house, but it was no problem finding him. All I had to do was whistle and he was never far from scrambling across the carpet, up my leg, and onto my head. But as Smokey grew more curious and rambunctious, Dad suggested I teach him how to be a real squirrel.

I began taking him outside and holding him up to see the other squirrels in the yard. Then I stuck him to pine trees, where he clung like Velcro. Despite my poking him in the rear, he was reluctant to go any higher. As further encouragement, I made a squirrel-like nest for him in the flower box beneath my bedroom window. From then on he slept outside, but I woke each morning to him still exactly where I'd left him, staring at me through the window glass with anticipation.

While Smokey wasn't interested in climbing trees, he seemed more than eager to help me test my critter traps. I had a variety of box traps I'd made out of plywood. A wire trigger in the back of the box served to release a trap door on the front. While testing one of these traps, the door slammed down on Smokey's tail and broke it. It eventually rotted and fell off, leaving him with a two-inch nub that twitched and wagged like a miniature greyhound. From then on, Smokey was scared of my critter traps, but he didn't seem to mind his new tail. And I got to put the rotten piece on a string and wear it as a necklace.

After a while, Smokey began to venture out of the flower box and explore the yard while I was at school. Mrs. Brodbeck was a kind, quiet lady about my grandmother's age living two houses way. She wasn't aware of my pet squirrel. One morning Smokey spied her sweeping the back porch in her nightgown. Always eager for human companionship, he sprinted across her yard, ran up her leg, and sought the familiar comforts of her head.

When I returned from school that afternoon, Mom reported that peaceful Mrs. Brodbeck had almost flogged herself to death with a broom trying to get a crazy, tailless squirrel out of her nightgown. Dad suggested I make another attempt at encouraging Smokey to adopt the ways of other squirrels.

We began our training again, and this time Smokey seemed more willing to participate. After a couple of days, he'd climb a few inches up a pine tree, turn a few circles, and go around the side. After a week, I could stick him to the tree and release him like a racing hamster. He'd shoot twenty feet up in a rain of pine bark and run out on the first limb he came to. Then I'd whistle and he'd turn around and come back to my shoulder.

Once Smokey grew comfortable climbing trees, he began to spend even less time in the flower box. Until one morning I woke to find him gone. I came out of the house and whistled for him. To my relief, I heard branches swishing and bark flying and hickory nuts falling. He was soon on my shoulder, where I let him stay awhile before sticking him to a tree again and watching him race away.

But gradually his mind grew foggy of me and clear with his inclination to become a real squirrel. At first I noticed that he took longer to come when I whistled. Then he would come halfway down a tree and stop and get confused. Then he stopped coming altogether.

For years afterward I stood in the yard and whistled and watched the squirrels in the trees. They all looked the same, but sometimes Smokey would twitch a little at his memories of me and give himself away. Then I studied him until I saw the nub tail and knew for sure that my friend was still with me.

HURRICANES

UNTIL I WAS NINE YEARS old, hurricanes were fun. School was canceled and nothing ever seemed to happen except for a little strong wind and rain. Then I experienced Frederic.

My siblings and I spent a long, boring morning watching Mom pack our clothes and food while Dad hurried around outside, bringing furniture off the wharf and nailing boards over the windows. That afternoon he sent us ahead to stay with friends in Stockton. He remained to finish boarding the windows and assured us that he would be along later in the evening. He tells me, all these years later, that what happened that afternoon is the only time he's ever felt he was in the midst of true evil.

Dad hadn't yet boarded the windows in the front yard. In Point Clear, most people call the yard near the water the front, even though that's not where the cars and the main entrance are. Also important to note is the fact that the houses were close together where we lived, forming a sort of wall between the bay and the back highway. In winter, the north wind can be howling at the front windows while the highway is still and peaceful.

After we left, Dad continued nailing plywood over the front windows. By late afternoon, the sky was dark and the storm surge already had the water lapping at the top of the bulkhead. He heard the wind in the tops of the pines, and looking out past the end of the wharf, he saw waves whitecapping far offshore. But it was calm where he was, and rain was barely falling. He had just a couple more windows to go.

Dad finally finished and hurried into the house to grab his suitcase. Once inside, he noticed the back windows were shaking and pasted with wet pine straw and leaves. He opened the back door and windblown rain hit him like lead shot. It was like stepping into another world.

A hurricane resembles a giant circular sawblade rotating counterclockwise. As Frederic made landfall at Dauphin Island, its wind came from the east, the top of the sawblade hitting the backs of the houses in Point Clear and diverting over their roofs to stroke the water again far offshore.

Dad had been shielded from the strengthening storm the whole time he'd been working in the front yard, tricked into a false sense of safety. Now, he discovered that Frederic was directly over him.

He made his way to the car and pulled out onto the deserted highway. As he drove up the road, he felt the wind rocking the car while the wipers whipped at the swirling sticks and leaves. When he got to County Road 32 and turned east, he watched in his rearview as telephone poles snapped and fell into the road behind him, sparks flickering white and blue and orange through the rain-blurred night. He even had to navigate around a few that fell in front of him.

"It was like the Devil was after me," he said.

Dad eventually made it to us in Stockton. And he didn't tell me that story until recently when I asked him what he remembered of Frederic. He felt foolish then and still does now.

When we woke up the next morning, it looked like a bomb had gone off outside. Days passed before the roads were cleared and we were able to make our way south again. When we finally got home, there wasn't a pine tree left standing in the yard. I thought it looked like a giant had crushed them beneath his feet like blades of grass. Pieces of people's houses and docks were wedged into the debris. It didn't seem possible to clean it all up.

I slept in my room that night with a pine limb that had punched through the roof hanging over my bed. We went ten days without power. Since the electric pump on the well wouldn't work, Mom boiled water from the bay to use for washing. We had clean drinking water in the bathtub, which Dad had filled before we left. Our meals were limited to powdered milk and canned food. But I was just a kid and it was all an adventure to me.

In the days that followed, Dad worked on clearing the trees. My siblings and I shoveled mud and sand out of the yard in hopes that a little of the St. Augustine grass smothered beneath would survive. For months afterward, the crisp winter air was filled with the sounds of chainsaws and trucks. It was heavy with the smell of briny bay water and diesel and two-cycle oil. And slowly, like a place swarmed with worker ants, the trash disappeared and our house stood on a leafless land of brown, not to be green again until spring.

Of course, now I dread hurricanes. I've even found myself envying friends with lake houses. Though I wouldn't trade my life on the Gulf Coast for anything, the sounds of chainsaws in the cool fall air never cease to remind me what a precarious foothold we have.

JOE

ACROSS THE BLACKTOP IS A vast wetland of tall pines, briars, and pitcher plants. When I was ten years old, I found a dog back there and named him Joe. He was a straw-colored mutt, a runty mix of yellow Lab and pit bull. I always assumed he'd wandered through the woods from a community of run-down houses a couple of miles east of us. He reminded me of the dogs I'd seen tethered by their leashes to clotheslines in bare-dirt yards. I imagined a runaway slave, escaping a miserable life of abuse and boredom. There were the pink welts and scars that showed through his short hair. There were the remnants of crazed fear that hung liquid in his eyes. If I moved too quickly around him or raised my voice, he grew skittish and tense.

When I think of boyhood and dogs and dog stories, I think of Joe. Since then I've had other dogs, better looking, more expensive, and with more personality. But Joe was there at an impressionable time in my life when I was learning how to go about being a man.

Most of the people in Point Clear moved back to Mobile in late August. The blustery southwest wind coming over the bay died off, and the days grew calm and quiet and cool with light breezes from the east. Dove cooed and fluttered in the treetops. With my summer friends gone, I turned my focus on the woods behind the house.

Almost impenetrable and full of ticks and poison ivy in the summer, in winter the soggy thicket was a quiet retreat from the cold north winds howling over the bay. I spent many days hauling an endless supply of driftwood from the beach and into the woods for making bridges and tree forts and animal traps.

I fed Joe at the house, but he lived outside and roamed freely. He usually appeared to me somewhere between my back door and the woods. He stayed with me throughout the day until it was time to go back inside for lunch or supper. Then he sat in the yard and waited for me to come outside again. If I didn't return after a while, he'd trot away to wherever it was he slept at night.

Even though Joe couldn't talk, and didn't seem much interested in what I was doing, he followed me about like he'd been assigned the simple duty of reminding me that I wasn't alone. And I was never happier to have his companionship than the first night I spent in the woods.

I was ten years old and I'd been thinking about it for a couple of years. Thinking that part of being a man was facing my fears and spending a night solo in that vast, mysterious thicket. On the designated day, I left the house as the sun was setting. Before I reached the highway, Joe had fallen in beside me. When we arrived at the tree fort, I shoved him up onto the tarp-covered platform I'd built about six feet off the ground. As the forest grew dark, I lay there staring at the underside of the tarp, trying to calm my fears. Joe was curled up beside my sleeping bag, and the rising and falling of his stomach against me was comforting through that long night of eerie sounds and boredom.

That night in the woods is the last time I clearly remember being with Joe. One day, not long afterward, I crossed the highway alone. I had not made it far into the trees before I heard tires squealing behind me. I ran back to find a car pulled into the ditch and Joe lying on the roadside.

His eyes were open and there was no blood, but I knew instinctively that he was dead. I was upset and I didn't want to touch him. I backed away and ran home to tell my father. I found Dad reading the newspaper in our living room and told him what had happened. As my younger siblings were also very attached to Joe, he decided it best not to tell them immediately.

"Go bury him before they see him lying there," he said.

I suppose I expected Dad to take over at that point, but he made no move to help. I went back outside to our tool shed to get the shovel and the wheelbarrow. I returned to the highway and carried Joe back into the woods, where I buried him in the same place I'd found him three years before. The task wasn't pleasant, and I was still upset, but I felt I was doing a man's job for the first time in my life. That final payment was a tough one to make, but it was time for me to learn that friendships and love come at a cost.

GONE TO TEXAS

I COULDN'T IMAGINE WHAT OTHER people did in summer without Mobile Bay to entertain them. I assumed they were all in a holding pattern somewhere boring until they could visit me. Since I lived in Point Clear year-round, I was a default playmate for many of Mom's friend's children when they came over from the city. I was also on standby to entertain the children on Dad's side of the family when they dropped in from Texas. My typical impression of most out-of-towners was tennis shoes that needed to be discarded immediately, a brand-new bathing suit that needed to be cured in muddy bay water, and a tiresome fear of catfish and crabs. It seemed I had to teach them everything.

When I was ten years old, Dad felt I needed to expand my horizons.

"Texas?" I said. "What's there to do in Texas?"

"Get to know your cousins. Experience life on the ranch."

Dad gave me a refresher course on my Key cousins and told me again of spending his childhood summers with Uncle Dave, a cattle farmer in East Texas. I wasn't listening. All I could think about was missed fishing and swimming. I pictured hot, breezeless cow pastures thrumming with cicadas and scum-covered watering holes.

Uncle Dave met me at the airport. He owned a dusty pickup truck and dressed like a cowboy. He drove me to the ranch, where I'd stay at Cousin Swan's house. She had two sons, who were about my age.

Luke and his younger brother, Michael, were standing in their driveway waiting for me. They were dressed in cowboy boots and Western wear. Luke was my age and, like me, on the small side. I vaguely recalled him visiting Point Clear once.

We faced off in what felt like a showdown.

"What you wanna do?" he finally said.

"I don't know," I said.

"He can ride in the football," Michael suggested.

"You wanna ride in the football?"

"*In* it?" I asked.

Luke's eyes shimmered with victory. "Come on," he said. "I'll show you."

I followed them inside the house and upstairs to what they called the play loft. In the center of the room was a giant plastic football. Luke sat on the floor and began kicking and beating on the top of it until he finally got it loose. Then he turned it over and poured out a pile of miscellaneous toys. Michael rolled it upright again and both of them stood back and looked at me.

"Get in," Luke said.

"What for?"

"So we can roll you down the stairs."

"Serious?"

"Yeah," he said. "Michael, you show him."

Michael eagerly climbed into the football. Luke pounded the top on again, rolled him to the staircase, and pushed him over the edge. The football bounced like a Ping-Pong ball, hit the bottom, and slammed into the wall. Luke ran after it, pried the lid off, and Michael crawled out smiling.

"See," Luke said. "We do it all the time."

At this point, I was convinced that my cousins weren't challenging me. They were offering their best entertainment, Texas-style. It took a few minutes to get me crammed inside and balled up with my face between my knees. I felt their fists and feet on the top of my head as they banged and stomped the lid tight. Then everything was dark and stuffy.

"Ready!" came Luke's muffled yell.

"Yeah," I muttered.

At first it wasn't so bad. Just gentle rolling. Then it felt like I'd been dropped off a cliff. Twenty times. The football was thinner than it looked and I felt the edge of every stair tread hammer me in the ribs . . . shoulder . . . head . . . rear end . . . kneecap. I didn't know how I'd survive. Just when I thought it was over, I slammed into the wall below and almost puked. I heard them running down the stairs and waited while they rolled me around and worked the lid off. Finally I felt a whoosh of cool air on the top of my head and saw glints of light beside me. Luke pulled on my neck until my head popped out of the hole.

"You like that?"

I took a deep breath and looked at him. "Sure," I lied. "What else do you have?"

"Let's ride the calf!" Michael said.

"Ride a calf?"

Luke was already out the front door with Michael behind him. "Yeah!" he called out. "We got some new ones!"

I caught up with them at the pasture gate. Luke had a bucket of what looked like giant dog food in one hand and a stick in the other. He started banging on the metal gate with the stick. Before long, cows began lumbering toward us. Michael climbed over the gate and stood in the pasture and Luke followed. "Come on," Michael said.

Luke dumped the food pellets on the ground and the cows clustered around them. Then suddenly, he took off running. After a second, I saw he was headed for a calf standing a little outside the herd. He jumped on its back and lay down with his feet around its stomach and his arms around its neck. The calf took off like a racehorse and made straight for the trees.

Luke was gone.

I looked at Michael, speechless. He kept his eyes on the pasture and pointed for me to watch. I did. A second later the calf tore out of the trees again, flying Luke from its neck like a scarf. When the calf passed close, Luke let go, rolled across the ground, stood, and brushed off.

"Try it!" he exclaimed.

I started running. I leapt onto the back of the calf and clutched it like a wet cat. For a few seconds everything was a bucking blur with the wind roaring in my face. Then I knew the calf was no longer under me. When I hit the ground, it felt like I'd been slapped on the rear with a board. Then my face rolled through something soft and slimy. Finally I came to rest, staring up at the clear Texas sky.

In a moment, Luke and Michael stood over me.

"You like that!"

Again, I was speechless.

They helped me up and Luke began brushing me off. "We can go swimming," he said. "Get you cleaned up."

"Swim?" I said.

"Yeah, you know how to swim, don't you?"

As it turned out, there was a lot to do in Texas. I ended up having one of the best weeks of my childhood with Luke and Michael. And learning that the world didn't revolve around Point Clear.

THE BIRD NEST

"I'VE GOT AN IDEA," I told my friend Jeremy. "We'll build a nest. A huge one, way back in the woods in the top of a tree. And we'll spend the night in it like giant birds."

"Okay," he said. He was my guest. What choice did he have?

I could think of no reason why it wouldn't work. I imagined us in a soft mat of pine needles high in the tree canopy, gazing up at the stars.

My mother wasn't worried about two twelve year-olds pulling an all-nighter in the woods across the highway. When the bay was windy and rough, I spent most of my time over there anyway. And I'd spent nights alone in my tree forts with Joe before.

It was late spring and already hot. But I knew we needed jeans and long-sleeve shirts and waterproof boots to go where I had in mind. A place I'd never been. As far back into the woods as we could get. Where I imagined no one had been since Indians. There was no telling what we'd find.

After lunch, I lent Jeremy some of my extra hunting boots. We each had a pocketknife, flashlight, and sleeping bag. For food, we packed two cans of Vienna sausages, some crackers, and a canteen of water. Then I snuck Dad's machete out of the tool shed and we raced for the trees.

We soon found ourselves in briar tangles that had us on all fours. Our boots filled with muddy water and our jeans caked in mud. We crossed shallow ponds, wading through pitcher plants, in black water that rainbowed with strange marsh oil. Sweat dripped in our eyes, and our boots sloshed hot and wet. But I was certain no one had ever gone so far. Not even Indians had made it into such a place.

After several hours, we broke from the dense underbrush into some relatively open pines and cane.

"We made it," I said.

The sun was just slipping below the canopy when I found the perfect tree. A large pine had fallen and hung so that it rested at a 45-degree angle. It was just right to walk up and get into the top.

"Up there," I pointed. "Let's start making the nest before it gets too dark."

We spent an hour cutting and hauling pine limbs and cane up into the tree. As the frogs began to cheep, we carried up armloads of pine needles to cushion our nest.

The woods slipped into twilight and I began to feel uneasy. I couldn't stop studying the dark shadows falling around us. We decided the bird nest was complete and hauled our sleeping bags into the tree and spread them out on the giant cushiony platform.

I felt better once we got off the ground to safety. We ate our Vienna sausages and crackers, sweaty and proud.

After dinner, we lay on our backs and stared at the sky. The stars weren't out yet, but the pine boughs rocked gently above us.

"We did it," I said. "A real bird nest."

"Pretty cool," Jeremy said.

"Nobody'll ever find it way back here."

We lay there quietly, thinking about it all. After a minute, I heard a dog bark.

"Where'd that come from?" Jeremy asked.

I felt the back of my neck tingle. "I don't know," I said. "Must be a wild dog."

"Wild dog?"

"Yeah . . . but they can't climb," I assured him. "Nothing can get us up here."

Darkness fell and I trained my eyes on all the strange sounds pressing into us. There wasn't much to do or talk about. I was nervous about moving or making any noise anyway.

The dog barked again. I sat up and looked behind us. I saw a light through the branches.

"Jeremy," I said. "I think I see a house."

He sat up and looked. As we trained our eyes on the dense tangle of trees, we began to make out more lights. Then we heard a screen door slam.

"Somebody came outside," Jeremy said.

My scalp tingled. Our eyes stayed locked on the lights. Then one of the lights flickered a bluish color.

"What's that?" I said.

Jeremy didn't answer.

In a few seconds, familiar music reached our ears.

"Sounds like *The Dukes of Hazzard*," I said.

"I think that's your house," Jeremy said.

All of my fears dissolved instantly, replaced with an overwhelming sense of defeat.

"We didn't go far at all," I said. "That's my sister watchin' *Dukes of Hazzard*."

We both turned back and lay down again. Frogs cheeped. Cicadas buzzed. The stars still weren't out.

"But we walked for hours," I said.

Jeremy didn't answer me.

"You like *Dukes of Hazzard*?" he finally asked.

"Yeah. You?"

"Yeah."

"You wanna go watch?"

"If you do."

I sat up. "I guess. It's pretty hot up here anyway."

DIRTY JOBS

WHILE POINT CLEAR CAN SEEM idyllic, there are activities going on behind the scenes that guests never see. As a youngster, I dreaded these dirty jobs that came with life on the bay, but I didn't necessarily think them unusual.

First and foremost in my memory is the grease trap. I didn't get suspicious of this particular duty until I was in my early teens and starting to complain about it to my friends.

"Don't you hate having to bail the grease trap?" I asked them. And they looked at me like they didn't know what I was talking about.

"What's a grease trap?" they said.

I assumed their parents hired someone to do it while they were at school. I described to them the cement tank likely buried outside their kitchen window, designed to catch everything draining from the sink. At least once a year I had to dig down to the cement lid, attach a block and tackle to the piece of rebar that served as the handle, and hoist the lid into the air to uncover a foul soup of greasy waste. Then I had to use an empty paint can to ladle the filth into a five-gallon bucket and haul it across the highway into the woods. There is no way to do this without gagging as it sloshes all over you.

My friends studied me. "We definitely don't have one of those," they said.

I eventually discovered that people with city sewers didn't, in fact, have or need a grease trap. I further discovered that most people who do have a grease trap don't have to bail it often, if ever. Like septic tanks, these mechanisms have a field line that is supposed to take the waste material out of the tank and leach it into the soil. Ours was simply not designed for a family of nine.

On to the dead things . . .

There is a never-ending supply of dead things that float up on the beach and have to be carted away like roadkill. Most of the smaller creatures can be removed with a shovel and deposited into the trusty five-gallon bucket. But we also find alligators, porpoises, and other large things that have to be towed out by boat.

Strangest of all were the cats. I consulted a neighbor.

"Do y'all find a lot of dead cats on your beach?"

"No."

I thought about it. We didn't encourage cats to stick around, but we certainly had more feline hobos than our neighbors. Our house was raised about two feet off the ground, and our central heating system ran beneath the floor. There were few families living in Point Clear in the wintertime, and not just cats, but raccoons, possums, and other critters traveled long distances to nest about the ducts for warmth.

But I'm still not sure how the cats ended up in the water.

Wintertime also holds other dirty perils. When I saw Dad bundled up and hurrying about the yard at night with a flashlight, dripping faucets, I knew there would be broken pipes in the morning. Even after you install a makeshift skirting of wharf boards, a north wind coming across the bay always seems to find a way to lick at the pipes until they burst. Repairing the copper lines involved squeezing under the house on your back in a puddle of muddy ice water holding a propane torch in one hand and a flashlight in the other. The spiderwebs didn't bother me as much as the tiny reflecting critter eyes and their hissing complaints.

Repairing the bulkhead was also done in wintertime when the tide was low. After pulling the waterlogged, scum-covered boards out of the mud, we hauled them off before they began to stink like more dead things. Then we used a water pump to sink the new boards and pilings into place. The entire project was done trudging in wet, cold, soupy mud.

Summertime had its own dirty miseries.

"Don't you hate tarring the roof?" I asked.

"What are you talking about?"

I learned that most of my friends were not familiar with roll roofing and the buckets of tar needed to install and repair it. All these years later, I still find it impossible to deal with roofing tar and not get it on myself. Even if you aren't required to be on all fours, spreading it with a paintbrush, I believe it can jump out of the can on you. The only way I knew of to get clean was to wipe myself down with gasoline.

Of all the chemical threats, creosote was the worst. This black toxin covered our pilings to keep them from rotting and we dealt with it summer and winter. Usually we wore long-sleeve shirts and long pants into the water and covered our remaining exposed skin with Vaseline, especially our faces. But the rainbow-like slick left on top of the water always seemed to find a way to get to our skin. The smell and chemical burn it leaves are so familiar to me that they've become nostalgic.

Actually, I suppose it's all a bit nostalgic these days. But I'm not one to chase ghosts.

THE GRAND HOTEL

POINT CLEAR HAS ALWAYS PROVIDED a quality of life that allows it to stand on its own, but the Grand Hotel makes it famous. As a kid, whenever I was outside the state and an adult stranger asked me where I was from, I proudly told them, "Point Clear, Alabama."

Typically, this had no effect on their expression.

Then I added, "On the coast where the Grand Hotel is." That usually did the trick. They'd likely heard of it or even been there.

Built by F. H. Chamberlain in 1847, the hotel was originally constructed as a two-story building with forty rooms. Despite a period of service as a Civil War hospital, numerous fires, hurricanes, expansion projects, and changes in ownership, the hotel has been known since its founding as the "Queen of Southern Resorts."

The hotel is not only a successful business, but also a valuable asset to the community, one that has always held Point Clear to higher standards. With its beautiful golf courses, immaculate lawns, fine dining, and well-groomed clientele, it has been a model of what the area deserves and what its neighbors should aspire to emulate. No matter what your own social standing is, you are always "not far from the Grand Hotel."

In summer, the morning calm is typically broken when the eastern breeze swings into a southwest wind. The fish have stopped biting and the fishermen are gone from Zundel's Wharf, a cluster of deteriorating pilings that have been a local fishing hole for decades. Waves begin rolling onto the beachfront. The cicadas begin their electric thrum in the wet heat. Before noon locals begin trickling toward the hotel.

It's an easy walk or bicycle ride if you live on the Boardwalk. Even easier for the kids that live in Lakewood. If you were like me, living south of Stone Springs, you had to journey by boat and park in the marina.

The hotel has always made an effort to include the community. We felt it was as much our resort as anyone else's. And on any summer day, it seemed there were as many locals roaming its grounds as true guests. The giant pool, rumored to be the largest man-made pool in the South, was the biggest draw. If you were a kid in Point Clear looking to meet up with everyone else over for the summer, the "Pool" was the place to go.

Parked out front were the first Porsches and Ferraris we'd ever touched. Inside the fence was where many of us got our first swimming lessons. It was my first experience with a high dive board. And as we strutted poolside with our hotel towels, the same ones they gave out to the guests, it was our time to feel like one of the "rich" people.

Along with its social benefits, the pool also provided many of us with our first jobs. Some of the local teenagers worked as lifeguards or grounds help. I was fortunate to get work at an early age. When I was ten, I talked the snack bar attendant into employment as the fly killer. She gave me a washcloth and I slapped flies and collected them in a paper cup. My flies were valued at ten cents apiece. When I had a dollar's worth, I cashed them in for lemonade.

My position as fly killer was eliminated by the health inspector (so they said), but I didn't take it too hard. Unemployed again, I went back to doing what most of the other kids my age were doing at the hotel: making friends and mischief.

We soon tired of smuggling live crabs from the bay to the pool and expanded our activities outside the fence and onto the main grounds. There were giant largemouth bass in the lagoon that needed catching and ducks and geese that needed chasing. Guests were always surprised to answer their door to a room service tray heaped with a rotting, fly-covered channel cat we'd found washed up on the beach. The first time we snuck into the lobby and stood in line for high tea, they shooed us out. It didn't take us long to realize that all a person needs for fancy cookies is a shirt, shoes, and shorts that aren't dripping wet.

If we were really bored, we'd walk out to Julep Point. The bay is always rough and treacherous off the point with a piling that reads DANGER RIPTIDE. In fact, the water is only a few feet deep. A person can easily wade out to the piling, grab hold, let the current sweep your feet out behind you, and start screaming for help. That will usually stir up excitement.

We knew the security guards by name—or at least by the names we gave them. Cranky Pants and Sunglasses and Barney. They patrolled in golf carts and weren't as fast on their feet as we were. Even if they were to catch you, it was rumored they'd just call your parents to come get you. I was never caught. Looking back, I wonder if anyone was ever caught. Maybe local kids making mischief is part of the allure of the hotel, an establishment so deeply woven into the fabric of its community that the lines between guests and locals are blurred.

THE JUBILEE

As summer slips into the heavy heat of July and August, afternoons on the bay turn rough and windy. By one o'clock, magazine pages are aflutter. Glasses of sweet tea are iceless and rolling with sweat beads. Flags ting-ting on their poles and pelicans ride the air currents just over the pine trees.

For adults, it feels like nap time. The children's mouths are stained with Popsicle juice and they want to keep swimming. But there's a thunderstorm crossing the bay from Mobile. You can hear the rumble of it and see the gray curtain of rain approaching. It's much faster than it looks. Within ten minutes, everyone is running up the wharf with raindrops spotting the boards at their heels.

After the storm passes, frogs cheep from the wet lawn and the waves beyond are left beaten into smooth swells, lapping against the beach. Cicadas thrum at the onset of evening. The air is so still you can hear the throbbing of a ship's diesel engine in the channel. A screen door slams ten houses away. Voices on the wharfs again. Lightning bugs . . . jubilee.

Combine a late afternoon squall, calm evening, and incoming tide, and you'll have the perfect setup for a jubilee. These conditions create oxygen-depleted water in the bay, which drive flounder, shrimp, crabs, and other bottom-dwelling sea creatures to shore. There can be anywhere from three to fifteen jubilees in a given year, most of them falling between July and September.

When I describe a jubilee to my out-of-town friends, they usually look at me with a skeptical smirk. I try to offer proof, but the pictures I have are blurry night shots. And due to their rare and unpredictable nature, it isn't the sort of event I can simply take them to. I have to accept that jubilees will likely remain a phenomenon that only people living on the Eastern Shore are able to truly appreciate.

The fish swim to the beach in the early morning hours when it's still dark. Like D-Day, they come in waves. I remember standing halfway out the wharf, watching flounder the size of large skillets gliding below me. I tried to throw the gig at them like a spear, but it never worked.

Schools of baby catfish swarm by the thousands. I threw my cast net over them once. I spent the rest of the morning trying to pick them out until Dad shook his head and told me the net was ruined. Another time I thought it would be interesting to jump into the midst of them. They stuck to my heel like sand spurs. My feet were sore and swollen for days.

As a child, I always thought the trout fishing would be good during a jubilee. I reasoned that if there were so many compliant fish near the beach, surely our fishing holes were full of eager trophies. I decided to be clever and take my skiff to Zundel's pilings while everyone else was on the beach. I never had a bite.

There's only one practical, painless way to get in on the action: go to the beach with everyone else.

The sea creatures crowd the shoreline and appear to be drugged and sluggish. There is little challenge to gigging the flounder or scooping the shrimp and crabs. They usually stay for an hour or two, then leave at daylight when ship waves come crashing in from the ship channel and stir the water. As if they've been shaken to their senses again.

The people who check for jubilees regularly get up several times a night and walk out to the beach and inspect the water with a propane lantern. The soft gaslight penetrates better than a normal flashlight. They look for crabs swimming on the surface, eels, fish with red bellies, and a general unrest of small bay creatures. If they see a jubilee developing, they'll usually go inside and call one or two of their neighbors. These neighbors come out with their lanterns and check for themselves. Once they're convinced a jubilee is moving in, they'll notify the people on their list. A chain reaction occurs until the waterfront is full of heavy footfalls on wharves. Shadowy figures wander the beach in their pajamas, the glow and hiss of propane lights floating up and down the shoreline.

When I was sixteen, my brother and I filled a rowboat with flounder and sold them to the Blue Marlin restaurant. It was the easiest money we'd ever made. These days I'm more responsible about how much seafood I take. Besides, I'm more interested in watching the kids enjoy themselves. I remember the fun of collecting samples of all the different types of fish that come in. We made exotic aquariums and tried to keep them as pets. It wasn't until we were a little older that we figured out why our fish never lived more than an hour or two. We'd made their aquariums out of jubilee water, just the thing that they were trying to escape. We'd jubileed them to death.

Though I've probably experienced a hundred jubilees by now, I still find them fascinating. And it's certainly an event that you have to see to fully appreciate. Unfortunately, unless you live on Mobile Bay, you probably won't see one. You'll just have to take my word for it.

SHRIMPING

DAD WOKE ME BEFORE DAYLIGHT and I followed him out into the damp, quiet morning. I was sleepy and my senses were dull. My first sensation was the feel of cool, wet grass slipping between my toes. Then the sound of the wharf boards pounding heavily under our feet. I was on the verge of wanting to be back in bed, but I never quite thought it. I wasn't excited, yet neither did I feel the excursion was optional. Even at a young age, there was something about the ritual that I inherently knew had to be done. Done because I was a boy and he was my dad and these were simply things a father and his son did.

I waited at the end of the wharf while Dad stripped to his underwear and waded out to the piling to retrieve our Stauter, a popular locally made wooden boat. He'd tied it there the previous evening when low tide and a southwest wind had left the water too shallow and rough to get it into the boat lift. Now the bay was heavy with high tide and the boat floated with a slack rope on water as calm as a lake.

Underway, I sat on the front seat and felt the breeze in my face and listened to the steady groan of the outboard trying to put me to sleep again. I watched the ends of the wharves go by. A few of them had lights on. Occasionally I heard the whine of a boat lift that needed greasing. More fisherman we'd see out somewhere that day. All of them going after speckled trout. All of us keeping score and not admitting it.

Fishing in Mobile Bay is primarily about the trout. If someone says, "He is a good fisherman," you assume he is good at catching trout. Everything else, even redfish and flounder, is what you catch if you can't catch trout. By-product. Consolation fish.

Dad slowed the Stauter near the Grand Hotel.

"Take the wheel," he told me.

I kept the motor at an idle while he worked in the stern untangling the shrimp trawl. A moment later he had the net and tickler chain out behind the boat. Then he positioned the boards on either side of the boat and organized the towropes at his feet. Finally he dropped the boards over the gunnels, one at a time, bracing and balancing himself against the ropes in a way I couldn't imagine ever growing into. The lines fed out through the stern cleats and occasionally he held them tight and I felt the Stauter surge against the net. I'm worried that I'm doing something wrong. It all seemed precarious and dangerous and surely catching something as small as a shrimp shouldn't involve this much effort. But he doesn't say anything to me, lost in his private struggle.

I knew the net was set when he let go of the ropes and they popped tight against the cleats. The stern dipped down and the boat was pulled to a standstill. Dad turned and moved toward me and I got up and let him take over again. He eased the throttle forward until the motor was groaning heavily and the Stauter eased through the water, straining against its work.

Dad had told me how the net operated. I visualized the mouth of it being towed behind us, the top lip held open with a line of corks and the bottom weighted with lead. The boards, a little forward of the net, spread the mouth into what I imagined looked like a whale shark. And between the boards dragged the tickler, a loose length of galvanized chain designed to scrape against the muddy bottom and alarm the shrimp into jumping up into the mouth.

There is nothing more monotonous than pulling the trawl. But if we don't have shrimp, we might as well go home. We've caught trout on artificial lures, but nothing compares to live shrimp. A trout fisherman feels an immediate loss of hope without them.

There were two more boats now, trawling quietly on either side of us. We could only see their navigation lights and the silhouette of their hulls, but we knew who they were. They were good friends of Dad's, and even within speaking distance, but we might as well have been separated by a mile. Everyone goes quietly, sleepily, and competitively about their work. But I knew that we'd already won a few points and a small amount of respect for being out there first.

After fifteen minutes, Dad started a wide turn near Slaton's wharf and the trawl ropes angled and dripped with tension. The sky was getting a pink glow to it over the tops of the pines in the east, and my stomach was growling. To distract myself from hunger, I tried to guess where we were going fishing. I sensed Dad working all the variables in his head: tide, wind, rumors. But I knew it would be one of only a few regular spots. They'd been productive for generations: the Grand Hotel, Zundel's, or Point Clear beacon.

Dad slowed the boat. It was time to pull the net. He went to the stern, gathered both towropes, and began pulling and coiling them in wet slaps at his feet. I remained seated, out of his way, but anticipation crawled over me. He got the boards in and started drawing the net over the gunnels. There were a few small croakers and catfish clinging to the mesh, but the bulk of our catch would be down the throat of the net, in a bulbous sack at the end. And it's not until this sack comes dripping out of the water that you really know how you've done.

"Get the washtub," he said.

I hurried to the washtub and pulled it next to him. Now was my opportunity to peer over the side and watch the sack appear. I could tell by the strain on Dad's arms that it was full of something. Then I saw it come from the water heavy, bulging, and dripping with moon jellies. He hefted the sack over the gunnel and dropped it into the washtub. Then he untied a small rope at the base of the net, lifted it from the tub, and our catch spilled into a puddle. Shrimp, croakers, catfish, eels, hogchokers, and one stingray all swimming in a gelatinous soup of moon jellies. I grabbed the bait net and began scooping the shrimp and dumping them into the bait well while Dad dealt with the stingray. Neither of us said anything, but we knew we'd done it right, each in our own way. And no matter what we ended up catching, we were that much closer to being men.

DOVE HUNTING

THE FIRST SIGN THAT WATERFRONT activities were over came to me as
the sounds of doves cooing and fluttering in the tree limbs. Then I began to take more notice of the cool breezes coming over the bay and the
water calm and clear like it was resting from the chaos of a long summer. And I began to accept the impending winter months with mixed
feelings of melancholy and excitement. Like something big was over
and next big thing had yet to start.

Dove season always seemed to arrive too early. It felt to me like
something men did only to pass the time until deer season. It lacked

the long road trips up the country and the adventures that came with spending the night at the hunting camp. There were no big woods and the weather wasn't as harsh. It was just an afternoon thing, a mild warm-up for hunting real, big game.

Dad would load his sons into the green station wagon and start up County Road 32 and into the farmlands of Baldwin County. In Summerdale were several fields we hunted with the same men that were in our deer club.

We met at a farmer's house around noon, parking under a grove of pecan trees. The men talked casually among themselves, leaning against their vehicles and occasionally bending down to pick up pecans and crack them in their fists. I never knew or cared what the grown-ups talked about. The kids were more interested in exploring the cavernous, dusty barns where the giant tractors loomed over us like sleeping beasts. To us, the highlight of the afternoon was dashing about the farm equipment until being told it was time to hunt.

A few miles up the blacktop was a small grove of pines standing out of an otherwise bare field. Everyone expected a good hunt if we were going to the pine tree field. Anywhere else was a backup plan.

To reach the grove, we turned onto a boggy dirt road that took us through a cattle gate and alongside a sinister swamp. The last person was to close the gate behind him to keep the cows in. As the oldest of the sons, I rode in the front passenger seat. Dad was probably the least enthusiastic of the dove hunters, and our car was typically last, and it was always left to me to close the gate.

"Watch out for the bull," he said.

There was always a bull. Every dove field we hunted was threatened by an angry bull that I never saw. And if I asked any of the other men about this, they never failed to deliver a story to back up Dad's claim. Always along the lines of somebody I didn't know getting chased by this monster and ultimately running naked across the field after having his clothes torn off by a barbed wire fence.

Of course, the pine tree field bull lived in the nearby swamp. All of them lived hidden in the most fearsome places.

The hunters set up their dove stools and mesh blinds around the grove. I was always happy to be on the side away from the swamp. I figured I would hear the bull kill the other men behind me and have time to run and squeeze through the barbed wire without losing my clothes. But sometimes I drew the unfortunate stand with only a small strip of pasture between me and that dark tangle of underbrush. And if I shot a dove, it would fall in the intervening space. Hurrying to retrieve it, I imagined the bull standing just out of sight, tensed up and watching me, waiting for me to stray too far.

The dove hunt was a lonely thing. There was no one to commiserate with about the bull. Everyone sat quietly alone, just out of speaking distance, watching the sky. Other than the occasional popping of shotguns, and the faint sounds of someone's portable radio broadcasting a football game, there were only breezes in the tops of the pines. Occasionally I had visitors, but no one I wanted to see. If another person strolled my way, I knew I was about to get "dumped on." When the more successful hunters approached their limit for doves, they "dumped" part of their cache among the rest of us so they could continue shooting. Not only was it humiliating, but I knew they'd never want those birds back. And Dad, consistently stubborn about eating what we killed, would require us to clean and eat them. I didn't like the taste of doves. And I didn't kill those things.

It was usually dark by the time we got back to Point Clear, our dove stools filled mostly with other people's kills. We plucked the birds on the end of the wharf, an icy north wind trailing feathers over the waves and our hands stiff and trembling. It seemed there were no lights for miles. The waves were rough and black and mean. It went against nature to be out there. Nothing about dove season ever fit. It started too early and ended too late. And left me wondering what exactly I'd gotten out of it except a heightened fear of bulls.

THE NECKLACE

MANY BOYS CONSIDER KILLING THEIR first deer a necessary step to manhood. And oftentimes the celebration that follows is as memorable as the hunt itself.

Sunday afternoons at the deer camp always left the woods feeling empty and lonely. I was twelve years old, and it was the last hunt of the weekend. Many of the club members had gone home that morning, but some of my friends had already killed their first deer and I was determined to take advantage of any opportunity to join their ranks.

Dad led me to a tree stand in a hardwood bottom alongside the Alabama River. There he left me with his .30-30 Marlin rifle and assurances that he would be back just after dark.

As the sun slipped low in the trees, I saw nothing but a few squirrels bouncing over the forest floor and some robins pecking in the leaves. An armadillo snuffled past and a possum climbed down a far-off oak. Then dusk was upon me, and the squirrels and robins disappeared and grew still. Three deer appeared like ghosts slipping through the hardwoods. I shifted the rifle in my lap and began to tremble.

It wasn't until they were nearly beneath me that I heard the faint sounds of their footfalls in the leaves. At first I thought they were all does, then straining my eyes, I saw small yellowish spikes on the head of the second one. I raised the rifle and tried to find it through the scope. Working against the grainy darkness and my shaking arms, I found what I thought was its shoulder, held my breath, and squeezed the trigger.

The rifle shot echoed for miles, shattering the silent river bottom and leaving me breathing hard and worried that I'd missed. Then I saw the white of the deer's belly lying not far from me. And I figured I'd just become a real man.

It wasn't long before Dad returned and stood over the deer, sharing my own mixed feelings of pride and disbelief. Then we pulled it out of the woods and waited for the rest of the hunters to arrive. A few minutes later, all of the men stood about on the dirt road, admiring my small buck in the headlights while I swelled with accomplishment.

"I guess it's time we bloody him up," Mr. Walter said.

I'd witnessed this ritual for years and had long prepared for the moment. Mr. Walter cut open the buck's stomach, stuck his arms inside, and came away with bloody hands. He wiped them over my face and all the men laughed and I was proud.

"We have to make him the necklace," Mr. John said.

I looked at Dad with question. I hadn't heard of the necklace. He shrugged and grinned like he, too, was enjoying it all for the first time.

Mr. John knelt beside the buck with his knife and cut off its testicles.

"Take out one of your bootlaces," he told me.

I did as he said and gave him the string. In a moment he had the testicles strung around my neck.

"Now," he said. "Everybody'll know. Got to wear the necklace."

I didn't question it. They could have told me I had to climb inside the deer and I would have. I wanted to participate in whatever they suggested to the fullest extent.

Typically everyone is anxious to get home Sunday evening. However, Dad said we needed to stop at Delchamps to get a few groceries.

And Mr. John and Mr. Walter said they needed to purchase a few things, too. I thought this was unusual, but I was eager for any opportunity to make a public appearance.

As I strolled the aisles, I saw other men and mothers and their children staring at my necklace. I figured they all knew exactly what it meant. And I imagined the looks on their faces couldn't have betrayed more envy.

After the grocery store, the men decided to stop at Wal-Mart and take care of some early Christmas shopping. It was still November and I'd never known Dad to holiday shop more than a few days ahead of time. Nonetheless, I couldn't believe my good fortune. I followed them about the store, walking tall, meeting the stares of the patrons with a steely confidence. The men didn't seem to find what they were looking for, but I found plenty of what I wanted.

That night I washed the dried blood from my face and climbed into bed still wearing the necklace. It wasn't long before Dad came to check on me. He studied my trophy and chuckled.

"I'm proud of you, son," he said.

"Do I wear it to school tomorrow?"

"Well, I think it was just for today," he said.

"*Can* I wear it to school tomorrow?"

He leaned over and took it off me. "I better put it someplace safe," he said.

I didn't know where he put it, but I assumed it was the same secret stash where my best art projects and other memorabilia went.

A few years later, I had a younger friend in another deer club who killed his first deer. To my surprise, when I asked him about his necklace, he had never heard of such a tradition. It occurred to me that a deer testicle necklace was part of a bygone era. That perhaps I had been the last kid to wear one. It later occurred to me that I might have been the first as well.

THE GHOST OF ZUNDEL'S WHARF—A LOCAL LEGEND

A TYPICAL POINT CLEAR MORNING in October finds light, cool eastern breezes filtering through the pine trees, brushing Mobile Bay into a glassy calm. Occasionally the breezes will gust in small patches and ripple the surface. Seagulls glide overhead and pelicans float as if they've slept on the water all night. It is still and quiet. It was on such a morning in 1938 that seventy-nine-year-old Augustus Stile was found in his rowboat at the foot of Zundel's Wharf. His wooden skiff gently bumping against the shore. He was speechless and his hair had turned white from terror.

Until the 1930s, there was no practical means of getting from Mobile to Point Clear by automobile. Everyone traveled by steamboat to Zundel's Wharf, a landing long enough to access deep water several hundred yards out and substantial enough to support railcars for off-loading supplies. At the base of Zundel's was a general store and post office. This was the small community's hub of commerce and transportation.

The wharf was constructed from giant creosote pilings and heavy timbers. In the days of steam, such heavy construction was dangerous business, especially when done over the water from rocking barges. This work was typically done by black day laborers. There were many deaths building these wharves, some from crushing injuries and others from drowning.

It is not clear exactly what Augustus saw the night before he was found. It is generally believed that he had an encounter with the restless soul of a long-dead construction worker, but we'll never know. He was only able to tell pieces of the story before a strange death overtook him.

Augustus was a descendant of an old Mobile Bay family. He had lived near the landing for several generations. The hurricane of 1916 destroyed the original wharf, leaving a long line of black, stripped pilings stretching far out into the bay. To this day, those pilings are still a landmark and haven for trout and redfish. Seagulls and pelicans use them as a convenient resting spot when their stomachs are full from the small fish that school around it.

Augustus's custom was to row his boat to the end of the pilings not long after sunset and fish for trout. He usually returned by nine or ten o'clock that night. One night he didn't return. When he was found the next morning, sitting motionless in his beached rowboat, Augustus's family was unable to draw him from his deep state of shock. They took him to the house of a local physician, who advised rest. Several days later, Augustus lost the glaze in his eyes and turned to his wife.

"I saw something out there," he said.

The family leaned close.

"What do you mean?" they asked.

Augustus told them he had anchored near the end of the pilings. The moonlight came silver across the top of the water. It was so calm and still, the bay seemed like a pool of oil. A few pelicans slept on the tops of the pilings and you could hear their talons scratch the wood as they shifted and preened. Occasionally he heard a screen door slam or a dog barking from the shore.

"He climbed out of the water," Augustus began. "He was wet and slick like a newborn baby. Like a shadow. Barely a ripple. But he was a man. A tall, thin man as black as ink. He climbed up the piling closest to me. Maybe ten yards away. He climbed fast, more like a scramble. He perched upon it like a child—sitting on his heels with his knees hugged to his chest. He watched me. I heard the water dripping off him."

"Who? How?" they asked.

Augustus shook his head.

"How could a man swim that far? What was he doing out there?" they asked.

"That was no man," he replied. "No man could do that. But I heard the water dripping off him."

"Augustus," they said.

The old man turned his head away, stared at the ceiling, and the dull glaze fell over his eyes once again. For a week, his family tried to get him to speak or respond to them in any way. Augustus remained silent and still and alone with the horror that had poisoned his mind.

At the end of the week, he suddenly turned his head and looked at his wife. His eyes had grown wide and clear. She grabbed his hand and squeezed it.

In a dry, raspy voice, he said, "He's out there."

"Who?" she said, leaning close, putting her ear to his mouth.

Augustus's breathing grew heavy. It seemed he was about to say something else. He never did. Finally his wife backed away and studied his face. His eyes were wide and clear again. She squeezed his hand and he slowly shook his head. Then he stopped breathing and slipped into death, his eyes still open and full of terror.

Through the years, people have occasionally related their own stories of seeing something perched on a piling at the end of Zundel's Wharf. Something too large to be a pelican, yet in a place and posture impossible for a man. Certainly for a living man.

THE POINT CLEAR LIBRARY

MY MATERNAL GRANDPARENTS LIVED ABOUT a mile up the beach from my childhood home in Point Clear. Their home was full of strange curios for a young boy to ponder. Corn grew on the wharf in planter boxes. The house chimney had a sinister iron cleanout door at the base that clanked in the wind and held the bones of dead birds and squirrels. The "dungeon," my brother called it. In the backyard were pear trees with fruit growing inside glass bottles. Next to the pear trees was an old wooden boat planted with strawberries. But most fascinating of all was a thirteen-by-fourteen-foot building near the highway. A sign above the door read POINT CLEAR LIBRARY. Inside were ancient books stacked ten feet to the ceiling. In the center of the floor was a mahogany rolltop desk with a scattering of yellowed membership cards and an open, handwritten register as if the ghostly librarian had only just walked out. On a bench, leaning against a window, was an article from *Ripley's Believe It or Not!* declaring it the smallest public library in the world.

The library is still in the backyard of what is now my parents' home. The white and green trim exterior looks as fresh as ever. The rolltop desk is gone from inside, but the original books fill the shelves. On a table in the center of the room are the blank library cards and the register containing many last names I recognize.

Along with the *Ripley's* vignette are several framed articles on the library's history. According to a 1941 piece in the *Mobile Press-Register*, the library was established in 1920 out of a reading circle run by Mrs. Theodore Hurlbutt. The building was originally located on the south side of Zundel's Lane, facing north. Dora Zundel, whose home was nearby, was the first librarian. She opened on Saturdays from two thirty to five, but if a book was needed outside of those hours, all one had to do was knock on her door. Her house was also full of books, and if she couldn't find something to match your taste, she'd walk over to the library with you and open it.

The library had approximately twenty-four hundred volumes on its shelves. As Point Clear was mostly a summertime community, there were only twenty annual members, who paid one dollar per year. Nonmembers paid ten cents per book per week. Most of the books were donated, but the local ladies also held teas and luncheons to raise money for upkeep and a small salary for the librarian.

According to Mrs. Zundel, the most popular items were Westerns and love stories, with mysteries second and adventure third. She was proud that people from as far away as China had stopped by to borrow something to read during their vacation.

As television became popular in the '50s, the library's patronage dwindled until it was no longer feasible to keep it open. The building was eventually moved onto the grounds of the old Point Clear School, about a quarter of a mile east on County Road 32. There it slowly fell into disrepair until 1970 when my father moved it one last time.

"I remember walking down the boardwalk, holding my mother's hand, going to check out a book," Dad tells me. "Nobody had television then. People came over on the ferry for the summer and books were all you had."

Dad's Alabama summers were interrupted while he was away with the Navy. It wasn't until he married my mother, a girl he'd known from Point Clear summers, that he returned. He found the old library with its door swinging open and the inside vandalized.

"There was just something nostalgic about it," Dad continued. "It represented a bygone era. A slower time. I wanted to save it if I could."

Dad approached Dorothy Pacey about purchasing the building. Her sister, Colleen Brodbeck, had been the last librarian. Mrs. Pacey told Dad he could have the library if he paid to move it. Additionally, he could keep what remained of the library's money, thirty-five dollars stored in a cigar box.

The Point Clear Library was subsequently moved to my grandparents' home and onto my childhood stage. To this day, visitors stop by to remember the little building and look through the register for the signatures of family members. As with most old buildings, there are rumors that persist. Nobody's ever claimed the library is haunted, but some believe a list of the names of the unknown soldiers buried in Point Clear Cemetery is shoved somewhere between two books. Over the years, Mom has had calls from representatives of the Daughters of the Confederacy asking if she's located it. She says she hasn't and doubts such a list exists.

I say nobody's touched the books on those top two shelves in at least fifty years.

POINT CLEAR TENNIS CLUB

EMPLOYMENT OPPORTUNITIES HAVE NEVER BEEN great for thirteen-year-olds in Point Clear. After my position as fly killer at the Grand Hotel snack bar was eliminated, I found other employment watering and mowing the neighbor's lawn. But I despised yard work and desperately sought other opportunities with more upside potential.

One week Mom signed me up for a tennis clinic to broaden my experiences beyond boating and playing in the woods. I soon found the tennis court was where most of the cool kids were going in the afternoon when they left the hotel pool. Suddenly I felt like I'd been let in on a big secret.

I couldn't afford private lessons so I decided to approach Point Clear's second largest employer, Point Clear Tennis Club, about a job for my thirteenth summer. I figured the rest would work itself out.

"The Club" was started in 1976 by Point Clear resident and tennis enthusiast Nan Arendall. It was quick to become one of the premier tennis facilities in the South, boasting the only covered courts in the area. For many years, it was home court for some of Alabama's most promising juniors, some of which Nan sponsored to compete outside the region.

The Club was about a two-mile walk from my house, a journey that I would make many times before I got a driver's license. Jeff Combs, the tennis pro, agreed to credit me three dollars per hour to groom the eight clay courts each morning and throughout the day as players finished using them. When I had built up sufficient credit, Jeff gave me an hour-long lesson for twenty dollars. In this way I was able to get about two private lessons per week.

In addition to learning to play tennis, I also made friends with the other junior players there. But despite my efforts, I never rose above being something like the caddy who occasionally gets invited to play a round with the real players.

My eccentric grandmother from Texas heard that I was interested in tennis. She asked one of her friends in the know for a good tennis camp she could send me to. The next thing I knew, I was on a plane to Bradenton, Florida, for a two-week stint at the Nick Bollettieri Tennis Academy.

I soon found myself in barracks with about thirty other boys close to my age. Outside our windows was a long line of tennis courts. Aside from this place appearing more like boot camp than my idea of summer camp, everyone else seemed to have a lot more rackets than me.

The next morning, a group of instructors got us all together on the first court and fed balls to us while Mr. Bollettieri looked on. He was a silent, serious-looking, artificially tanned man in his mid-fifties. He wore dark sunglasses and drove a red Ferrari. He always wore a tennis outfit but I never saw him play tennis.

The instructors assessed our abilities and the more advanced players were moved down the courts with the most talented ending up at the very end. Finally it was just me and this boy named Bill left with one assistant, who didn't seem much older than us. Mr. Bollettieri had moved to the far court to watch a couple of our campmates, Andre Agassi and Jim Courier, hit with each other.

Over the next couple of days, the instructors videotaped our strokes and critiqued them on a movie screen like reviewing a football game. We were placed on a steady diet of water and fruit and grains and protein drinks. And Bill and I plunked endless tennis balls in the broiling Florida sun.

"What is this place?" I asked Bill. "I mean, I'm just the court boy at Point Clear Tennis Club."

Bill agreed that he, too, was in over his head.

"Man, these guys are way serious," I said. "They don't even talk to us anymore."

"No kidding," Bill said.

"We've got to at least get some real food," I said.

"How?" Bill said. "It's like a prison."

"I saw a 7-Eleven store up the road before they dropped me off. I'll bet they've got hot dogs or something. I'm gonna have to jump the fence on this place before I starve."

That evening Bill kept lookout while I climbed the chain link and hiked to 7-Eleven with the little cash I'd brought with me. I came back with a sack of Cokes and hot dogs. We sat on our bunks and had a feast while the others looked on in horror.

The next morning Mr. Bollettieri called us into his office. It was the first time he'd ever talked to Bill and me directly. He asked us if we'd like to be sent home. I started to answer yes, but Bill interrupted me and said, "No, sir."

So I stayed. And I hit more tennis balls. And more than ever I appreciated the easy slow-paced development of my game at the Point Clear Tennis Club.

A few years later, I began seeing some of my old campmates on televised tennis tournaments with Mr. Bollettieri watching them from the stands. I wasn't a bit envious. I knew what they had to eat to get there.

ARRIVAL

WHEN I WAS FIFTEEN, I told my father that I wanted to work construction. He suggested I get in touch with Kenny Horton, who lived down the beach about a mile. He wasn't certain what it was that Kenny built, but the man had a beat-up truck full of tools and lackeys that coughed by every morning.

After the last day of school, I set off down the highway on foot and walked the mile to Kenny's mailbox. The beat-up truck was in the driveway and Kenny was sitting alone on the tailgate drinking a Coors. He watched me like he'd been waiting on me.

I walked up to him and stood with my hands in my pockets and we watched each other for a full five seconds before he finally said, "Yeah?"

"I'm Watt Key. I was wondering if you needed somebody for a summer job."

"I always need somebody."

"How about me?"

"You know how to work a chainsaw?"

"Yes, sir."

"Jet pump?"

"Yes, sir."

"Be here at six Monday morning."

"Yes, sir."

That evening I found Dad in the living room reading a book.

"Dad, we still got a chainsaw?"

"Yeah."

"You know where I can get a jet pump?"

He looked up and eyed me. "I know where you can rent one. Why?"

"I need you to show me how to work them before Monday."

Monday morning I stood before Kenny's truck at 5:45 a.m. At 7:00, he came out of his house and walked past me with a cup of coffee. He stopped at the end of the driveway, looked both ways, and came back. He shook his head and looked down at me. "I guess you'll have to do," he said.

We drove to Fly Creek Marina that morning. Kenny didn't say anything to me as he rubbed his temple and sipped his coffee. I leaned against the passenger door and smelled the sweat and spilled beer and rust of real men and their tools. I breathed in the cool, wet morning air coming through the window and all of it swelled me with pride.

We parked in front of the Yacht Club, and Kenny told me to get the hose to the jet pump and follow him. He lugged the pump itself and I trailed with the accessories around the side of the restaurant and up the edge of the marina. We stopped before an older, tin-roofed section of boat stalls and Kenny set the pump down. He walked out on the dock and stared at the black water that rainbowed with leaked fuel.

"Jump in there," he said.

Had it been a hundred feet to a boulder pile instead of six feet to an oil slick, I would have gone. I never imagined such places with a bottom, yet as I swirled in a tannin world of metallic sound and water that tasted like hot seaweed and bug repellant, my feet pressed mud.

When I broke the surface, Kenny studied me. "I didn't mean it literally," he said. "You want a rusty nail in your foot?"

"No, sir," I said.

He shook his head. "All right then, take the end of this jet hose and be careful."

We sank a piling that day and it was the beginning of two seasons I spent with Kenny and his lackeys. I drank my first beer that summer and learned about wife problems and money problems and drinking problems and more wife problems. Kenny liked me because I was always on time and he knew he was my hero and I'd work myself dead for him.

The second summer he bought a sailboat and put it on blocks in the marina. He left me to sand and refinish the wood and patch the blisters in the fiberglass. It was the most pleasant work I can remember. I arrived early when everything was beaded with dew and the crunch of clamshells under car tires was the loudest thing in the marina. I'd lie on my side sanding and painting and watching the morning play out in the harbor. Most times Kenny brought me lunch and checked on my progress. Some days after lunch I'd stretch back out on the deck of the boat and sand and paint until the sailboat masts started plinking to the late afternoon breezes. Some days he let me knock off early and I'd ride with him to check on other projects he had going. I was his sidekick and everyone knew it, especially me.

When I finished the boat at the end of summer, Kenny and his girlfriend took me and a girl I knew from school sailing out to Gaillard Island for an evening cruise. We listened to Jimmy Buffett and drank beer, and I've never been prouder than I was then. I had arrived.

POINT CLEAR TOWING

POINT CLEAR NEVER HAD A town center or even enough year-round residents to support a convenience store for long. Our local characters were limited to the postmaster, Mr. Metzger, and Pete Nelson, who owned the general store a half-mile south of us. The rest of our characters we had to import. If you had a fire, you called the Barnwell Fire Department. Police, call Fairhope Police Department. For a tow truck, call "Mad Bill Dickson."

Mad Bill was a cranky white-haired man my grandfather's age. I'd seen his truck pass and I'd heard my mother talk about the one time she'd had to call him.

"Lady, you must be the stupidest woman I ever met!" he said to her.

He grew into a legend to us kids. Bill Dickson was *always* mad.

Before I got my driver's license, I was riding with an older friend through downtown Fairhope. I saw his tow truck pull to a stop at an intersecting street ahead. It was like spotting a celebrity.

"There he is!" I said. "Mad Bill Dickson!"

My friend wasn't from Fairhope. "Who's that?" he asked.

"I'll show you," I said.

We were just about to pass his tow truck when I leaned across the seat and tapped on my friend's horn. One might think Mad Bill was shot in the butt with a BB gun. He was on his horn before ours even sounded, hair-triggered with a sixth sense for mischief. Horn blaring, he erupted into a muted cursing frenzy from behind his window glass like someone gone insane in an aquarium. My friend swerved wide into the other lane, terrified. The sound of Mad Bill's horn fell away behind us.

"Wow," my friend exclaimed.

"I told you," I said. "You don't *ever* want to call Mad Bill."

I'd had my driver's license a week. My friend Archie and I found ourselves at my house, pondering rumors of the older boys from school tailgating somewhere near the Fairhope Airport. I had a vague sense that I needed permission to go driving around the countryside at night, but my parents were out for the evening. Besides, it was just a bunch of farm roads out there. How dangerous could it be?

When we started east on County Road 32, it began to rain. And after about thirty minutes, we gave up on finding the party. I turned onto another blacktop and started toward home. We hadn't gone far before the asphalt suddenly ended and we found ourselves fishtailing out-of-control on a rain-slicked dirt road. A moment later we were sunk to the chassis in a muddy, freshly turned potato field.

Even if my parents had been home, the last thing I wanted to do was call Dad for help. I didn't need this on my record after only a week.

We hiked back up the sticky road to the distant light of a farmhouse. The woman who answered the door said she had no way of pulling us from the field. Before I could stop her, she was calling Bill Dickson.

"We're dead," I told Archie.

Thirty minutes later we were back at the car, watching the tow truck turn off the highway and start our way. I had a sick feeling in my gut. I wondered if he remembered me from the horn incident.

Bill got out and stood in his headlights, shifted his pants, and greeted us. "How in hell did you manage this!"

We stood quietly while he winched us back onto the dirt road and wrote out a ticket and gave it to me. Thirty-five dollars. It was only then that I realized I didn't have any money and neither did Archie.

"Can we charge it?"

"Charge it! Charge it to what?!"

"I don't know. Like Fairhope Hardware. Like pay later."

Bill Dickson leaned close to me and said. "Boy, let me tell you somethin'. That money better be in my mailbox before sunup or I'm callin' the police."

I nodded. "Yes, sir," I said. "No problem. Where do you live?"

He turned and stomped toward his tow truck. "Figure it out!" he yelled over his shoulder.

As we made our way back to Point Clear, I began to appreciate the challenge that lay before me. I had to get home, somehow come up with thirty-five dollars, somehow find Bill Dickson's mailbox, get back home, and wash the car before my parents returned.

I was certain that if I didn't pay Bill Dickson what I owed him that night, he was going to have me arrested. We searched the house, scraping every bit of change we could from beneath the sofa and out of Dad's change box. We came up with about nine dollars.

Fortunately my older next-door neighbor was just returning from a date with her boyfriend. I saw their headlights sweep across the house windows. We crept outside and hid in the bushes until she got out of the car. I asked her if she had twenty-six dollars and she said she had some babysitting money she could loan me.

We found Bill Dickson's address in the phone book. A moment later, Archie and I were on the highway again. After some winding about in downtown Fairhope, we managed to find the mailbox, stuff it full of our cash, and pour in the loose change. Then we hurried home in time to wash my car and catch the opening credits of *Late Night with David Letterman* just as my parents came through the front door.

I'm sure Bill Dickson made a lot of people think twice before getting stuck again. I suppose it's healthy to be scared of the tow truck driver.

FIRST CARS

I ALWAYS ASSUMED THAT THE clandestine street racers I heard late at night originated from, or at least had connections with, the shade tree mechanic operations I passed on County Road 32. These racers played in my imagination like outlaws. Little did I know that a brief foray into that world would get me well on my way to being a successful teenager.

I had recently turned sixteen and Dad said he had a car for me. My grandmother's old sedan was parked in a barn at an abandoned farm in northern Mississippi. He thought he could get it running and bring it home.

A week later, I returned from school to find a '72 Oldsmobile Toronado parked in the driveway. It was a beige land barge with a hood like a dance floor. It had some dents and scratches, but it was mine, and I couldn't have been happier.

I drove the Toronado across the highway and parked it in the shed. My school friend Hank had painted his own car and I figured there was no reason I couldn't do the same. I started slapping Bondo over the dents and sanding it smooth. Then I went to the auto parts store and bought spray cans of primer and paint and went to work.

I soon discovered that you can't paint a car with spray cans and expect it to look like the new car I'd imagined. I needed an expert. And the closest place I knew of that seemed to work on old cars like mine was just up the road on County Road 32.

His name was BooBoo and he had a crude sign on a sheet tin building that advertised painting and auto body work. He was a man of few words. He looked over my project for a minute, then told me to bring it back on a full moon.

"Full moon?" I said.

He nodded. "I only paint at night on a full moon."

I told him I didn't know when the next full moon was, and he was fine with me leaving it with him and walking home.

For a couple of weeks, I went outside every night and looked up at the sky. Finally a slice. A half. Full. Two days later BooBoo called and said it was ready.

It looked like new, in an antique car sort of way. I had arrived once again.

Besides the paint job and the fact it was mine, there were other aspects of the Toronado I was equally proud of. It had a giant 455 V8 engine that roared like a beast chained under the hood. Back then it was all about spinning the tires and I could burn one to the radials in less than twenty seconds. The peculiar fact that it was front-wheel drive only added to the monster's personality. While my friends were spinning their tires and fish-tailing out of control, my machine hopped and clawed its way up the asphalt like an insane gold digger.

There was no end to the accessories. On the dashboard I installed the "button." It was something I found on a novelty rack in a truck stop. Just a plastic stick-on clicker that said TURBO.

"Don't ever push that," I told my passengers.

"Why?"

"Just don't."

They always hovered their finger over it, but no one ever pushed it.

I went to the junkyard and got a horn off an eighteen-wheeler, brought it home, and wired it under the hood. I installed a household light switch beneath the steering wheel to activate it. More fun. I was in love with my Toronado. I would die for it, and I soon found out that it would do the same for me.

One of my friends told me about an older model car he had that would backfire on command. He told me all you had to do was get going about forty-five miles per hour, turn the engine off for a few seconds and coast, then turn it back on.

I tried it, but I should have already known the old girl was going to give me her best. The back end of the car jumped and it sounded like the gas tank exploded. Black smoke and rust and bolts and nuts blew out the back end. Then a loud clattering commenced beneath the chassis like I was driving through a pile of scrap metal. Finally, I swerved free of it all and watched my muffler and tailpipe cartwheel into the ditch.

I took a deep breath and pressed the accelerator. She had a new voice. Now she sounded like a logging truck . . . Even better.

First cars. Oh yeah.

BASEBALL

WHEN THERE ARE ONLY NINE boys in your high school class, sports are not always optional.

My friend Archie approached me one day during lunch period.

"You want to play baseball this year?" he asked.

"No," I said. "I've never played baseball in my life."

"We need you. We've got eight players but we need nine."

"But I'm already doing cross-country and tennis."

"You can just come to practice a few times and show up for the games. None of them are on weekends and we get out of class early."

This was sounding better.

"What do I need?"

"We'll go to Wal-Mart after school and get a glove for you. We've got all the rest of the stuff."

"What about cleats?"

"You can just wear your tennis shoes."

Archie and I drove to Wal-Mart after the last bell and I purchased the cheapest glove they had. It was purple nylon with REGENT written on it. When we got back to school, I saw the rest of the boys gathered half-spirited at the corner of the soccer field, which doubled as our baseball field. Andy Burris seemed to be getting them organized. I assumed he was the team captain. Andy was the best athlete of us all and the captain of every team sport.

As we approached the group, I asked Archie who the coach was. He pointed to an old man sitting high above us on a hilltop, sipping from something in a paper sack. "Him," Archie said.

"Who is he?"

"I don't know. I've never met him."

The boys were relieved to see me and found new energy knowing they could finally field a team.

"Just stand out there in right field," Andy told me. "If anything comes your way, Hank will run over from center field and catch it."

"Fine," I said. "What about batting?"

"No problem," he said. "Just stand there and strike out."

"So basically, just stand around."

"Yep."

I was starting to like baseball. It sounded like I got to skip class to hang out with my friends and do nothing.

For a few weeks, I stayed after school, slipped on my purple glove, and hung out with the boys on the soccer field. Sometimes the coach was on the hilltop; sometimes he wasn't. He never said a word to us. Andy told me his name was Mr. Wasp, but I never heard him called that. I never heard anyone speak to him at all. But I shrugged it off and reasoned there were just a lot of things about baseball I didn't need to know.

Our first game was against Frisco City, a rural school in Monroe County. We got out of class about two o'clock and boarded the old ragged-out sports bus. I was surprised to see Mr. Wasp sitting behind the steering wheel. We filed past him and took our seats. Mr. Wasp closed the door and mumbled his first words.

"Big game, boys," he said.

The baseball field at Frisco City had no wall or back fence. Corn grew right up to the edges. And the Frisco team consisted of the biggest boys I'd ever seen. Farm animals. Most of them had mustaches and seemed like they should be fathers. They didn't smile at all and it was obvious they took baseball very seriously.

Our team spent most of the time in the outfield as the home team scored run after run. Most of their balls sailed or rolled into the cornfield and there was nothing to do but stand there and watch the runners lap the bases. I had a couple come my way, and if Hank could get to it, he would. Most of time it went into the field with the others.

Finally it came to be my turn at bat. By this time I was getting a little bored.

"You mind if I try to hit it?" I asked Andy.

"Sure," he said. "Why not."

The Frisco City crowd seemed to like it when I walked to the plate and picked up the bat. By now they were on to me.

"Hey, tennis shoe!" one of them shouted from the stands. "Hey, boy, gonna mess you up!"

I wanted to turn around and smile and explain myself. Surely they'd like me if I let them in on the joke. But everything was happening too fast. The pitcher was already starting to wind up. And then, suddenly, I heard the ball slap into the catcher's mitt and the umpire yelled so loud I thought I'd done something wrong.

"STRUUUUIIIKE!"

Holy crap! I thought. *No way in hell anybody hits that!*

"Come on, Watt," I heard one of my buddies laugh.

I didn't think it was funny. I was terrified of getting a hole in my chest the size of a grapefruit. The ball was so fast that I couldn't even follow it, much less try to get out of its way.

"How you like that, tennis shoe!"

I tightened my grip on the bat and braced myself for instant death.

The pitcher fired another white streak past me. I didn't know what was worse, the supersonic pitch or the umpire yelling at my face. I just wanted it all to be over. And in a moment it was.

On the ride home, I noticed the team didn't seem too discouraged. In fact, Archie told me the only time they'd ever won against any team was due to a forfeit.

As we filed out of the bus, Mr. Wasp nodded to us. "See you at practice, boys," he said.

Keeping to tradition, we didn't win a game the entire season. In fact, we didn't even come close. But sometimes you just have to take one for the team.

THE RUNAWAY

I WAS SIXTEEN YEARS OLD and I'd had enough. I was sick of chores. I was sick of curfews. Sick of all the questions about what I was doing and where I'd been. I was ready to cut ties and live the free life.

I was self-sufficient. I had a car and money from my job helping Kenny Horton. It was summer and I could sleep under the stars and be fine.

Saturday morning I was standing in the driveway beside my car when Mom came outside to get the newspaper.

"I'm running away," I told her.

She picked up the paper, stopped, and raised her eyebrows at me. "You are?" she said.

"That's right," I replied, savoring the bravery of my decision.

"When are you leaving?" she asked.

"Right now. I've got a tent in my trunk and I'm going to live on Fish River."

I watched her while she looked at my car and then back at me again. "Well, that sure does sound like fun," she said. "What kinds of things will you eat?"

"I'll catch fish," I said. "And I've got my own money to buy groceries."

"Is anybody coming to live with you?"

"Maybe," I said, like it was none of her business. "I've told some people I'm going to be out there."

"Do you want me to cook you something and bring it to you?"

"No, Mom. I don't want you to bring me any food. I'm *running away*."

"Okay. I understand. Gosh, I sure wish I could come. It sounds like so much fun."

She really doesn't believe me.

"So, I'm leaving now."

"Okay," she said, turning back to the house. "Have fun and let me know if you need anything."

I watched her walk inside and shut the door. I got into my car and backed out of the driveway, more full of angst and determination than ever.

They'll see. They'll be begging me to come home after I've been gone a few days.

I pitched the tent on the riverbank of a wooded lot my father owned. My friend Archie came over that afternoon. He wasn't claiming to be a runaway, but he was always up for a campout. We swam in the river and talked about girls and music and cars and freedom. Late that afternoon, we caught some small bream and made a campfire and cooked them. As we were picking the last of the fish meat off the bones, a Chevrolet Suburban pulled up.

"Is that your mom?" Archie said.

"Geez," I said.

Mom got out of the car holding a paper sack and her purse.

"Hi, Mrs. Key," Archie said.

"Hello, Archie," she said. "You boys sure have got things looking good out here."

I frowned and didn't respond. She held out the sack.

"I brought some sandwiches just in case you want them."

"We've already eaten," I said. "We caught fish."

She set the sack down. Then she took her camera out of her purse and began taking pictures of the tent and us by the fire and our paper plate of fish bones.

"The rest of the family wants to come visit you tomorrow after church," she said. "Your brothers can't wait to see your new home."

I couldn't take it anymore. I stood up.

"Mom, I'm running away. You can't come out here and take pictures and bring me food. And I don't want everybody coming to see me. This is *serious*."

"But it just looks like so much fun. Living out here on your own and catching fish and hanging out with your friends."

"It *is* fun. That's why I'm doing it."

"Just stand over there by the tent and let me get one more."

"No, Mom. Can't you just leave me alone?"

"Oh, okay. We're having steak tonight if you get hungry."

"I've got plenty to eat."

That night some more of my friends came by and we made the campfire bigger and turned up the car radio and drank a few beers and watched the sparks rise into the pine boughs. Life was good.

The next morning Archie had to go back to Bay Minette for church. I piddled about the campsite, picking up drink cans and restringing my clothesline, which somebody had pulled down. Then I sat beneath a pine tree and ate a can of cold Vienna sausages. When the cicadas began buzzing, I stripped to my underwear and went to sit in the river. I sat there, trying to dredge up the passion for independence I'd had the day before, but I just couldn't get to it. Then I thought about how hot it was getting. And it was Sunday and nobody was coming by to visit.

I can't go back now.

Why not?

I couldn't remember exactly what I'd been mad about. But there had been something.

Oh, well. I guess I showed them.

Satisfied, I began to take down the tent, already tasting the leftover steak at home.

INTO THE WILD

THE FIRST TIME I MOVED away from Point Clear was when I went off to Birmingham-Southern College. My main objective was to get this college thing out of the way without disrupting the finer sides of being a young man. Of the schools I applied, BSC was the closest to the bay and hunting camp, making it the obvious fit.

I soon found that most of the other students were more concerned with traditional education than hunting and fishing. Somewhat alarmed, I buckled down and tried to do the right thing. However, like any good Southern boy, I really just pined for the outdoors.

At BSC, they had a month-long term in January called interim. For most it was an opportunity for community service or additional study related to one's major. I learned that it was also possible to design your own course. Ever since I was a child, I'd dreamt of living in the woods like an Indian. I immediately saw this interim term as the perfect opportunity not only to do it, but to receive college credit for it.

In order to get my Indian course approved, I needed a college professor to sponsor me, then I had to develop a formal proposal to present to a panel of faculty for final review.

I approached my history professor after class one day in early November and presented my idea.

"I want to go into the woods wearing nothing but my underwear and live for two weeks."

He studied me. "And do what?"

I was surprised the idea needed more explanation. That it wasn't immediately the most interesting proposal he'd ever heard.

"Just live there," I said. "Try to survive like an Indian."

I approached a second professor and was once again rejected and dismissed for similar reasons. They couldn't find any academic merit in my proposal.

Optimism dwindling, I tried a third time with my young psychology instructor, Dr. Goodrich. I thought this was likely a long shot as she was from the Midwest somewhere and probably wouldn't understand a Southern boy and his desire for the woods. But she listened to my one-sentence proposal, and to my surprise, I saw a faint glimmer of interest in her eyes.

"That's a fascinating idea," she said. "But I think we need to work on your presentation of the concept before we send it to the interim board."

I finally had a sponsor. The rest, I assumed, would work itself out.

The rest turned out to be much more than I'd imagined. First of all, we revised my proposal to suggest a study of isolation for the

Psychology Department. And there would be required reading like Thoreau's *Walden* and several survival books.

Two of my college friends, Cheairs Porter and Sam Parker, soon got wind of what I was up to and told me they wanted to be a part of it. Once they were involved, modifications were made that included a full outfit of clothing, a limited supply of matches, and bows and arrows. I concluded these things were reasonable as it would be January and cold, we could find ourselves in real trouble without fire, and it could take us two weeks just to make a weapon. Otherwise we agreed to take no food, no water, and no shelter. Our extra items included a knife, axe, skillet, water bottle, cooking pot, poncho, and sleeping bags.

We submitted the proposal and waited. A week later Dr. Goodrich called and told me BSC had approved their first-ever survival interim course. We were going into the woods.

The day of our departure we woke at 5 A.M. in my house in Point Clear. Mom cooked us a big breakfast of bacon and eggs and biscuits and saw us off. By 7 A.M. we were 60 miles north at the end of a dirt road in south Monroe County. We spent another hour hiking under overcast skies into the Alabama River bottom swamp to a place I knew from previous hunting seasons.

We spent that first day building a palmetto and pine bough shelter in the rain, all of our gear soaking wet within the first two hours. Late that afternoon the rain finally stopped and darkness fell over the woods. I was concerned about sleeping in a wet sleeping bag, but I was growing more concerned about food. For the first time in my life, I was facing the possibility of going to bed hungry.

Like a gift from the heavens, I saw a cottonmouth, obviously washed out with the rains, making his way sluggishly through the leaves. I shot at him with my bow from about ten feet away. To our surprise, I hit him. It was the first thing I'd ever killed with a bow and arrow. And I thought, *This is going to be easy. We're going to live like kings out here.*

We skinned the snake and gutted him and placed him in our skillet with some rainwater. After much effort, we managed to find some wood dry enough to burn and started a fire. We watched the snake writhe in the boiling water (without head, skin, or guts) for what seemed like ten minutes. Finally the snake turned a pale color and appeared done. We cut it into lengths about the size of Vienna sausages and bit into the rubbery meat. The pieces flinched.

As we nibbled at our snake meat around the dying flames of the fire, night sounds pressed in on all sides. Despite a long, wet day, our shelter was mostly done and we were optimistic that we could spend the following day hunting and gathering food.

An armadillo waddled by and began blindly rooting in the leaves a few feet away.

"I don't care how hungry we get," I said. "There's no way I would ever eat that thing."

How hard could it possibly be to get food with animals all around us?

Journal Entry—Day 1

This is awesome. Indians had the life.

The next morning, our shelter complete, we decided to get serious about the food situation. Deer. Rabbits. Wild pigs. Bacon. I didn't know where the bacon was in a pig, but I was going to find it.

I wandered through the swamp that morning and came across six wild piglets, no bigger than dachshunds. I wanted something bigger, but decided I'd better come back with them just in case no one else's hunt was successful.

That evening we had piglet for supper. We boiled the meat in our cooking pot. It wasn't much, but we made the most of it. We ate the livers, brains, and even singed the hair off the skin and made crackling. The next day I found three more of the piglets. Once again, it turned out to be all we'd have for supper.

"Bacon," I said. "I've got to find the bacon."

But the piglets were so lean, the only fat we could get was from licking the inside of the skins. We were all starting to crave fat.

JOURNAL ENTRY—DAY 4

Leftover piglet for breakfast. Getting weak now. Time to start eating acorns until I can find the bacon.

>*Recipe for acorns:*
>*Shell acorns.*
>*Boil to get tannic acid out.*
>*Strain through sock you've been wearing four days.*
>*Repeat to taste.*

>*Recipe for pine needle tea:*
>*Pull pine needles from pine tree.*
>*Boil to taste.*

JOURNAL ENTRY—DAY 5

Pine needle tea is actually pretty good. Acorns give you terrible burps. Sam is craving fried chicken. Cheairs wants a roast beef and provolone sandwich. I want lemon pie. And bacon.

The deer smelled us and ran. The wild pigs vanished. Our days were spent trudging through the swamp sailing arrows at whatever moved. We drank from puddles like dogs. We stared at the armadillo that nosed in the dirt every evening around our shelter.

"It can't be that bad," I said.

My friends were too weak to comment. I got up and killed the armadillo. I cut the shell off its back and dug out the oily, crimson-colored meat. It stank like nothing I'd ever smelled. I stir-fried it in the skillet and we forced it down. I knew it wouldn't taste good, but I never imagined it would be *that* bad. The stench stayed on our hands and breath for days.

. . . Until we discovered one could eat pine bark. Showing my friends it was okay, I mowed through a limb section about the size of a piece of silver queen corn. It tasted exactly like you think it would—like eating sawdust soaked with turpentine. We couldn't take much of it, but it cured the armadillo breath.

JOURNAL ENTRY—DAY 8
Pants are falling off. Have not used toilet paper in 9 days. GOD, I want some bacon.

It wasn't raining. The temperature dropped below freezing a few nights, but we could handle that. Water was plentiful. It was the lack of food that was really crippling us. We hiked to a small pond, dug up some larvae, and caught about a dozen sardine-size fish. I don't know what they were. We cooked them over a fire for a few seconds until we saw them starting to shrink. We jerked them out, chewed them up, and swallowed them before they disappeared.

JOURNAL ENTRY—DAY 10
Sam and Cheairs think this is the stupidest idea I've ever had. I told them there's no way we'll die. I heard a person can go a month without food.

JOURNAL ENTRY—DAY 12
Too weak to hunt. Still haven't used toilet paper. Friends not even coming out of shelter. . . . Think I'll crawl outside and lie in the leaves just so I can feel like I'm doing something.

JOURNAL ENTRY—DAY 13
Bacon . . .

We trudged out of the swamp at one minute after midnight on the fourteenth day. We went straight to Delchamps grocery store in Spanish

Fort—the closest and only place open at that time of night. We staggered through the automatic door like escaped POWs. We went our separate ways and met again in the parking lot and ate our fantasy foods in silence. We vomited. Ate again. Vomited. Repeat.

After we returned to school, no one doubted our effort. I'd lost fifteen pounds. We were all streaked with pine sap and infected cuts.

My friends were able to keep food down after a few days, but I still couldn't eat without it bouncing up again. Someone predicted I had contracted trichinosis from eating the pig livers. When word gets out at school that you might have worms, it doesn't help your social life. I immediately went to the doctor and got checked out. He said I didn't have worms, but my stomach had shrunk so much that it would take a while to stretch back out again. In a few more days I was finally able to keep food down. And Birmingham-Southern posted our grades for the interim term.

Pass.

THE BODY

FALL IN POINT CLEAR IS like a party that is over, cleaned up, and waiting until summer again. The air is quiet and cool. The eastern breeze keeps the bay calm and smooth, and doves coo in the trees and flutter about the yard. Schools of mullet ripple past the end of the docks, and speckled trout thrash the baitfish under seagulls not far offshore. Our Stauter boats are out of the cable lifts, turned over in the backyard on sawhorses. We'll fill the nicks with Bondo, sand them, then refinish the wood with Jack Tar paint. Now hunting season is on our minds.

Even though there are hundreds of acres of woods across the highway from our house, I don't recall any real hunting going on in Point Clear. In forty-plus years, I've never even seen a deer there. Back in the '70s and '80s, one could shoot skeet from the end of the wharf without worrying about a call to the sheriff. You could even fire off a few rounds from your new high-powered deer rifle and imagine the bullet landing somewhere out in that empty bay, maybe near Middle Bay Lighthouse. But there was hunting there before my time. Dad told me that his first test as suitor to my mother was standing in a pair of waders with a shotgun out near Zundel's pilings while my grandfather ran his Stauter in circles stirring up the ducks. The waders leaked and the bay was icy cold. He didn't get any ducks, but he passed the test.

So here we were, years later, a resulting family of nine planning for Thanksgiving dinner. The meal was quite a production in our household. But an even bigger production was getting back from the deer hunting camp in time to make it. My brothers and I always had to squeeze in that last morning hunt and hurry home.

One afternoon we were about to start without my brother Reid when I heard his tires crunching the gravel in the driveway. I met him outside as he stepped out of the old secondhand Cadillac my grandfather had recently sent to him. It still had the Texas plates on it.

"You get anything?" I asked.

"Yeah," he said hesitantly. "I got one. Big six point. But I shot it yesterday and didn't find it until this morning. That's why I'm so late."

"Where is it?"

"In the trunk."

"In the trunk?"

"Yeah. Come look at it."

I followed Reid around the car. He popped the trunk and I saw the buck lying on a blue tarp with ice bags stacked around him. I studied the scene briefly before the foul smell drifted over me.

I backed away. "That thing smells awful, Reid!"

"Yeah," he said. "I wanted to ask you about that. You think it's still good?"

"No."

"I couldn't even play the radio because it pumped the smell out of the back speakers."

"It's definitely bad."

"I didn't just wanna leave it. I shot it and all."

"You need to get rid of it before it ruins the car."

"What do I do with it? I can't just put a whole deer in the trash can."

"I don't know . . . I guess you can dump it off the Fish River Bridge."

"Good idea," Reid said. "Is that legal?"

"I don't know why it's any different than leaving it in the woods."

"Yeah. Good point."

"Or a dead fish."

"Yeah."

"Shut the trunk so Dad doesn't see it and take it after lunch."

After Thanksgiving dinner, Reid hurried off to dispose of the deer. He drove out to the Fish River Bridge and attempted to stop in the middle a few times before he realized there were too many passing cars to give him time to drag the body over the guardrail unnoticed. Then he had another idea. He recalled that not far away was a wooded lot my father owned on the river, one of the last undeveloped pieces in the middle of a new riverfront housing development. He reasoned he could park in the woods and drag the deer down to the water without making a big production of it.

Reid bulled the Cadillac through an overgrown trail until it petered out not far from the riverbank. After much effort, he managed to pull the deer out of the trunk, drag it through the brush, and shove it into the river. Then he returned to the car, leaned against it, and rested.

"Excuse me," he heard someone say.

In his exhaustion, Reid hadn't noticed that two men had approached from the house next door.

"Hey," Reid responded nervously.

They studied the blood on Reid's hands and clothes. The open trunk with the bloody blue tarp and rifle lying next to the spare tire. The blood swipes down the chrome bumper. The Texas tag. The blood and flattened grass leading away toward the river.

"What's going on back here?" they asked suspiciously.

Reid recontemplated the legality of dumping a dead deer. "Nothing," he said.

"What's your name?"

"Reid Key."

"Where you from?"

"Point Clear."

The strangers glanced at the tag again. They made a mental note of something and hurried away. So did Reid.

I'LLNEEDA

EVEN A REMOTE COMMUNITY LIKE Point Clear had its share of transients. Sometimes they arrived on bicycles, sometimes on foot with tall backpacks. They typically had good stories to tell, which was our price for a glass of iced tea and a roadside rest. Usually they didn't linger for long, but I remember two that pitched tents in our backyard and stayed several days. The most memorable was determined to make a new home in the woods across from our backyard.

My younger brother Murray announced that he'd found a witch.

"Where?" I asked him.

"In that fallen-down house in the woods across the road. She's all wrapped in blankets and stares at you."

I knew the old one-room shack he was talking about. The driveway into it was overgrown with pine trees, and the building was nothing more than a roof caved in over rotting walls.

"Whatever, Murray," I said, annoyed. He was known to have a large imagination, even for an eight-year-old. And as a college kid with a summer job, I had better things to do than go after imaginary witches.

It wasn't long before items started to go missing around the house. First it was canned food. Then it was pots and cups and dishes. Then one morning Murray called Mom and me into the kitchen and pointed out the window. Wandering about in our yard was a disoriented, disheveled woman in her late fifties, naked except for a blanket slung over her shoulder. Her hair was gray and stiff and looked like something birds had been nesting in.

"That's her," Murray told us. "It's I'llNeeda."

"Good Lord," Mom said.

"The witch?" I said.

"She's not really a witch," Murray said. "We're friends now."

"Her name is I'llNeeda?" Mom continued.

"That's what I call her," Murray said. "All she talks about is what she needs. Yesterday she said, 'I'll need a broom.'"

"Is that where my broom went?" Mom asked.

Murray nodded. "The day before that she needed cans of soup."

"Murray, is that where everything in my kitchen's been going?"

"She told me she needed it all," he said.

Murray introduced Mom to I'llNeeda that morning. While I was at work, Mom investigated and verified the woman was homeless and living in the old shack just like Murray said. She'd already eaten most of the canned goods Murray had taken her, but Mom was able to get her broom back along with several pots and pans and a flower vase.

"I'll need a dress," I'llNeeda told her before she left.

Mom took I'llNeeda a dress and a plate of food. A new friendship was formed.

I'llNeeda began coming over in the mornings needing coffee. To the horror of my siblings and me, it became routine to see Mom and I'llNeeda taking coffee together in the kitchen. I felt that I could see the stench rising off her like gasoline vapor. We estimated, in terms of years, how long it had been since she'd washed.

"Ten," Alice suggested.

"Twenty," Betsy said.

After coffee, I'llNeeda wandered up the highway into Fairhope. She spent the day on park benches telling passersby that she lived across from the Keys in Point Clear and had everything she needed there.

"Seriously, Mom," I said. "What's wrong with her?"

"I think she's handicapped. We're trying to find her family."

"This is crazy," I said. "She can't stay here."

"Well, it *is* a little embarrassing," Mom admitted.

With a light eastern breeze, our yard was sometimes enveloped in the smell and smoke of burning leaves. In an attempt to cook, stay warm, or both, I'llNeeda often built fires in front of the shack. They inevitably grew out of control and we'd find her shrouded in bluish smoke, beating at the flames with her blankets.

"Mom," I complained, "she's going to burn the woods down."

Parental duties were rarely shared in our household. It was either a Mom thing or a Dad thing. I'llNeeda was strictly a Mom thing for a good reason. Mom has a high tolerance for, and sometimes even encourages, absurdities.

One afternoon I got home from work to see I'llNeeda out the front window, standing naked on the beach. Murray was thrashing around in the bay in front of her.

"Mom!" I called.

Mom walked into the room.

"What's going on out there? I'llNeeda's naked again and Murray's with her."

"Oh, it's all right," she said. "She was washing her dress and a ship wave took it. Murray's just trying to find it for her."

Mom's inquiries into I'llNeeda's family finally led to a call from her son, who was living in Florida. He said that she had a history of wandering off and had been missing for months. He came and got her and moved her into a nearby assisted-living home.

Life around the Key household returned to normal, but we all felt a little loss after I'llNeeda was gone. Mom went to visit her and it made us feel better to hear that she had everything she needed at her new home.

MARDI GRAS

AFTER COLLEGE, I RETURNED HOME to live with my parents again in Point Clear. I didn't have a detailed life plan, but I knew I wanted to live in the bay area. And my new job as a computer programmer for a Mobile company seemed like a good start. My boss had even given me a cellular phone, in those days an expensive accessory that made me feel I was destined for great things.

While my professional life seemed to be on the right track, my social life was lacking. Now my college friends were scattered across the country and I'd lost track of my high school buddies. I was the youngest person in my office building and there wasn't much nightlife to be found in Point Clear. I went to work and came home each day, hoping that somehow the rest would work itself out. But little did I appreciate the eagerness with which Southern women will set about steering your social life for you.

I was coming home from work one evening, driving across the causeway, when I answered a call from Mom on my cell phone. She said my older cousin had gotten me into a Mardi Gras organization. Like Mobile's neighbor New Orleans, Mardi Gras is the defining celebration for the city.

"Should I do it?" I asked her.

"Of course!" she said. "Your grandfather and lots of your Mobile cousins are in it. It's lots of fun."

Unless Mom had put them up to it, I couldn't imagine how anyone would have suspected I'd consider a Mardi Gras organization. As a family, we'd never participated much in the carnival. Dad wasn't involved and we had always gone to Disney World during the break. I recalled going to only a couple of parades when I was a child. I held lingering memories of a cold, damp Bienville Square packed with people. Colorful confetti and tremendous floats moved under oak limbs in the wet dark, and hard candy rained down over me in impossible quantities. Then there was the memory of a giant, terrifying skeleton stalking me through a crowd. When he was looming overhead, he tilted up his mask and I saw another cousin's face behind it. The sensory impact of the experience was so overwhelming that it stayed with me almost dreamlike.

Considering my other social outlets, I didn't see the downside.

"Okay," I said. "Sure, I'll do it."

Mom told me my cousin's phone number and I called him and he gave me the time and place for my initiation ceremony. On the appointed evening, I met him outside the clubhouse, or "den" as they called it. Then he slipped a hood over my head and led me inside. As I suspected, the initiation ceremony was nothing more than about ten minutes' worth of silliness before I was unmasked and ushered into the crowd of onlookers. I immediately found myself amid more of my older cousins, people I knew only from summers on the bay and trips to the hunting camp. And I had a revelation that this was what they all did when they went back to Mobile.

I was one of the youngest men in the club. Over the months leading up to Mardi Gras, I went to the meetings and stood against the wall and soaked up the noise and chatted with the few people I knew. I didn't feel my social life had gained the traction I was looking for, but it was better than spending the evenings alone in Point Clear.

The day of my parade finally arrived and I left Baldwin County to make the journey across the bay and downtown, where I was to board my assigned float. While confident I was on the fast track at work, I still wasn't making much money. I still drove my grandfather's old F100 with a three-speed column shifter. While it wasn't much to look at, it had always been reliable. In fact, it was so simple that I'd never had anything go wrong that I couldn't limp home with.

Having misjudged traffic and the challenges of navigating downtown during the carnival, I soon found myself running dangerously late. I was somewhere in the mad ant bed of downtown when, in a state of anxiety, I snapped the shifter off at the column. I found myself in the middle of the street holding it before my face in disbelief. Cars were soon honking behind me and all I could do was rev the engine helplessly. I got out of the truck and dug around in the bed for a screwdriver. I soon found one, jammed it in the column, and managed to get the truck into second gear.

Unable to get out of second gear, I lurched and coughed and sputtered as close as I could get to my parade. Then I pulled up on a curb, shut off the truck, and started running. As I came close to the parade lineup, it appeared that it was leaving at any moment. The generators were already running and the floats were full of maskers. I rushed into the room where our costumes were hanging. Most of the racks were already empty and I couldn't remember exactly where my section was. Fortunately someone I knew came rushing through to get something he'd forgotten.

"Which one?" I asked him frantically.

"You're probably a pirate," he said. "Geez, you better hurry up."

"Where's all my stuff to throw?"

The man was already hurrying away.

"I don't know," he said over his shoulder. "They probably loaded it up already."

I grabbed the last pirate costume and got into it. It was so big that

I felt as if I'd been draped in bed sheets. Then I pulled on a mask and jammed on the pirate hat and bolted out the door somewhere in the middle of the lineup. The scene was already riotous with maskers, high above me, yelling and rocking the floats with anticipation. I hiked up my pants and searched for fellow pirates, but didn't see any.

I desperately looked about for assistance but everyone was masked and I didn't recognize a friend in the bunch.

"Where do I go!?" I yelled up at someone.

The man pointed dismissively up the line of floats and took another swig from a bottle. I held my pants with one hand and started running.

Vikings. Penguins. Cowboys. Eskimos. Until I was finally at the beginning of the line, staring up at a float full of fish.

"I don't know where to go!" I yelled up at them.

"Just come on," someone shouted.

"But I'm a pirate!"

"We *need* a pirate! Get up here!"

My first ride certainly got off to a bad start. I'd lost my family and had no throws. But once the marching band started beating their drums and the parade began to snake its way through a sea of cheering spectators, the incomparable thrill of celebrity fell over me. And there was one happy pirate dancing among the fish.

THE PERFECT POND

A COUPLE OF YEARS OUT of college, I was still living with my parents in Point Clear, but I was ready for a place to call my own. I didn't have the money to build a house, but I decided a small piece of land would be a good start. I soon found a wooded lot on Fly Creek with what looked to me like a shallow pond at the foot of it.

"Why has it been on the market so long?" I asked the real estate agent.

"Because of that . . . that swamp down there."

"You mean the pond?"

"Well, yes," she corrected herself.

This confirmed my suspicions that the price of the lot and the time it had been for sale were all because no one had my vision. I imagined a small house overlooking a fishpond where I could write and be like Thoreau.

After purchasing the property, I asked Dad to come over and advise me on some boundary line issues, but I really just wanted him to see the pond.

"Son," he said, "that's no pond. That's an old oxbow that's filled in with mud. There's nothing but snakes in it."

But I wasn't deterred. I came in the evenings after work and sat there and imagined all my pond could be. I watched snakes glide through its shallow, grassy water. Little minnows rippled the surface and turtles watched me from logs. Occasionally, when the creek rose, water back-flowed in and left small bass and bream to dart about the reeds. But it wasn't deep enough to hold them. It wasn't perfect yet.

That weekend I got a shovel and began to dig. My hands were soon blistered and my back ached from lifting the large chunks of gooey mud. At the end of the day all I had was pain and a pond full of ugly divots.

The next weekend I drove to the building supply store and rented a small backhoe. I managed to scoop a few shovel loads of mud from the very edges, but the arm didn't reach the middle. I realized my efforts were once again in vain and my pond even more scarred.

Twenty workers from Labor Finders digging for one day, I thought. *Can't afford that.*

A cable stretched over the pond with a clamshell dredge on a pulley . . . Where can I get a clamshell dredge?

A real backhoe like the kind I see building shopping centers on the four-lane . . . Tear up the driveway. Too many trees. Can't get it down there.

A trash pump! Yes!

I rented a trash pump and invited my younger brother to help me. We flopped about at the end of a fire hose for half a day, slurping chunks of mud and spitting them on the bank. But a trash pump requires you to suck a minimum of two-thirds water to keep it flowing. About noon the pump shut off and I wiped the mud from my eyes to see that I'd sucked my pond dry. The turtles were crawling away and minnows flipped about like little pieces of muddy glass. I quickly turned the pump around and pumped water from the creek back into it. By the time my pond was restored, it was late in the afternoon and all I had to show for my efforts was a giant puddle of chocolate milk.

A couple of months went by. All of my leads on clamshell dredges dried up. I was getting discouraged. Then I thought of the little track hoe sitting in front of the rental place. *Tracks!* I thought. *Something with tracks can go anywhere! I can drive it straight into the middle and dig my pond as deep as I want.*

I rented it and drove it in. I worked in a circle, scooping buckets of mud from around myself and dumping them on the perimeter. For a short time it seemed things were working, that my pond was becoming perfect. But all the while my track hoe was sinking inch by inch. Each shovelful of mud pulled it deeper. Then I realized that the muffler was gurgling. I tried to drive forward and the tracks spun. Backward, the same thing. I lifted the stabilizer arms and slapped them back down into nothing. I tried to pull myself out with the shovel arm, but the machine didn't budge. I tried everything at once, resembling a crazed-looking mechanical bug flailing for my life in a tar pit.

Eventually the engine went underwater and died. I climbed off with a sick stomach, dreading the phone call I was going to have to make. And it wasn't the rental place I was scared of; it was Mad Bill Dickson's towing service.

As Mad Bill winched the machine from the muck, he let me have it. I was the stupidest kid he'd ever met. If I were his son, he'd wear me out. If he were the rental company, he'd sue me.

Mad Bill left me standing in the yard next to the track hoe. It was pasted with mud and dead minnows, deep gouges down to the pond as evidence of what had happened. I didn't want to be there when the rental company retrieved it.

When I returned from work Monday evening, the prints of some larger piece of equipment were pressed into my lawn and the track hoe was gone. A bill was taped to my door.

It was years before my swamp was perfect again.

A NIGHT AT MIDDLE BAY LIGHTHOUSE

A FEW MILES OFF THE end of our wharf and a little to the left is Middle Bay Lighthouse, a famous Gulf Coast landmark since the late 1800s. We've been there many times, fishing the structure and climbing into it. Sometimes we jumped from the roof into the mysterious, spooky depths, where fear of your feet touching whatever was down there spiked white hot up your spine.

One night I was fishing in our old Boston Whaler at Zundel's pilings with two of my younger brothers, Reid and David. The bay was glass calm and the sky full of stars. Middle Bay Lighthouse glowed softly, beckoning us from the ship channel.

"Let's spend the night in it," I said.

They agreed. We'd discussed it before, but never done it. I had a suspicion that it wasn't permitted, but it was always open and seemed a harmless act. Besides, we planned to be out of there at daylight.

We went back to the house to get sleeping bags, pillows, and a few snacks. Finally, we woke Mom and told her what we were doing.

She was still half asleep when she mumbled, "Have fun."

We made the run to the ship channel and approached the lighthouse. Reid let David and me off on the ladder with the gear. Then he anchored the boat out and swam over. We helped him onto the ladder and started up.

I've often thought the structure belongs to seagulls more than people. The first thing one notices when standing on the deck is the overwhelming stench of bird droppings. The boards are coated with them, white and chalky and sticking to your bare feet like bits of wet clay. Inside, the lighthouse is eerily clean. None of the graffiti or trash or dust you would expect in an abandoned building. You'll find a couple of bare rooms with a spiral staircase leading to a small second floor and finally a ladder leading up to the roof, where the old light was originally mounted.

We spread our sleeping bags in one of the bottom rooms. Then we stayed up for a while, lying on our sides and fishing through a hole in the floor. We eventually went to sleep a little before midnight.

In the early morning hours, I awoke to the sound of thunder. The temperature had fallen a few degrees and the sweet smell of a squall hung over me. Before long, rain tapped at the windowpanes.

At first, the storm was a soothing addition to the adventure. But as the rain came harder, water ran across the floor and wicked into our sleeping bags. We were soon backed against the far wall, listening to waves crashing into the supports below and wind whistling over the building.

"Sounds bad out there," I said.

My brothers agreed. We took turns peering out the window, trying to check on the boat. But it was pitch black outside and we couldn't see a thing. Wet and cold, we waited helplessly for daylight.

As dawn crept over us, we saw Mobile Bay whipped into six-foot seas. I had never seen it so rough. Fortunately the boat was where we'd left it, rising on the wave crests and crashing down into the troughs. Although we were relieved, it seemed impossible that it wouldn't drag anchor. If we didn't get out of there soon, it was likely we'd be stranded.

We decided to go for it. On the deck, the rain blew at us so hard it stung our faces like lead shot. We finally gathered our courage and leapt out into the waves. After a brief struggle, we made it to the boat and climbed into the back.

Somehow we managed to get the anchor up. Then Reid and David sat on the deck and used towels and life vests to shield themselves from the rain. Meanwhile I started the engine, pulled my shirt over my head, and put my face up to the compass on the console.

East, I thought. *Just keep the arrow on East.*

I kept my face pressed to the compass, running blind, plowing through the storm. It was too rough to go more than a fast idle. Part of me was terrified and another part of me felt like a hero.

I gradually came out of the storm to find myself about a half-mile offshore and a few miles south of our house, near Mullet Point. The water before us was calm and gently rippled with an eastern breeze. Like the storm had been our private punishment.

"They'll never believe what it was like out there," I said.

We pulled up to the wharf, thoroughly beaten. I saw my mother running out. She hugged us all. She had seen the storm on the news that morning and remembered where we were and seen the boat missing.

Somehow we'd avoided the Coast Guard cutter and the flotilla of locals that had gone out looking for us.

Inside, as we were eating a big breakfast, the phone rang. Mom answered it. She listened for a moment and held it out to me.

"It's for you," she said smugly. "It's the Coast Guard."

Officer Thomas cleared up any questions I had about camping in the lighthouse. So you'll know, it was illegal back then, and it's still illegal today.

MAJORS CREEK

WITH GULF SHORES, MOBILE BAY, and the Mobile-Tensaw Delta, there's no end to the water-based adventures one can get into on the Gulf Coast. It seems I've dabbled in just about all of them, but when I sit back and reflect on what I'd most like to be doing on a free Saturday, I yearn for narrow tea-colored creeks running through the remote Alabama backwoods. I think of their cool swimming holes over bottoms of polished gravel and white sand. I imagine drifting shaded tunnels, using small tackle, casting the cut banks for bream and bass that you suspect have never seen a fishing lure.

When I was a teenager, my friends and I floated these creeks in the spring and summer with light aluminum jon boats and trolling motors. Places like Little River and the headwaters of Fish River. Then along came college and day jobs and marriage and kids. Float trips no longer fit into my schedule, but I never stopped daydreaming about them. And I was certain that when the time came, my young son, Albert, was going to find them just as memorable.

Albert was six when I decided it was time to take him on his first float trip. It wasn't long before I'd recruited two of my friends, Archie and Daniel. Archie also had a young son that he was eager to bring. We decided on our favorite route, Majors Creek, just north of Stockton.

It seemed a lot harder to get organized than I remembered, but I was packing for two now, and should have expected it. Fortunately I didn't hold anyone up. Archie and Daniel ran into similar delays, and by the time we all met at the Highway 59 bridge, it was nearly two o'clock in the afternoon. We left Archie's pickup truck there and took mine, loaded with our boats and gear, upstream to the bridge on Silas Ganey Road.

Before shoving off, I studied the creek using the satellite map on my cell phone. I saw a dark, lush green valley snaking what looked like five or six miles through the piney woods. I knew we'd be pushing it to get out before dark, but I didn't remember it ever taking more than four or five hours. And with daylight saving time in effect, we should be fine.

We started off dragging the boats down a gravel creek bed that was covered in only a few inches of water. I suddenly remembered this as being pretty common on these adventures, especially at first. As we got farther downstream, the water usually got deeper and quicker.

We were still in sight of the bridge when we encountered our first fallen tree spanning the creek. This, too, I remembered, was to be an occasional nuisance. We pulled over the tree and continued on. The bridge fell away behind us, and the trees closed overhead and we descended into the cool, dark shade of wilderness.

An hour later we were still dragging over gravel and we'd lifted our boats over at least fifteen fallen trees. Occasionally we encountered water more than six inches deep and excitedly jumped in our boats and began paddling, only to find ourselves out again fifty yards downstream. It was like a tornado had come through there. I didn't remember it being nearly so much work.

"When are we gonna fish and swim, Daddy?" Albert asked.

"I don't know, Albert," I said. "Maybe later."

By the time I found my first fishing hole, it was nearly four o'clock in the afternoon. I made a few quick casts just to complete that piece of the fantasy. Meanwhile Archie pulled out his cell phone and studied it to see how far we had to go.

"No reception," he said.

"We better keep going," Daniel said with a look of concern.

We didn't stop any more to fish. We didn't stop to swim. Eventually it became deep enough for us to use the trolling motors, but it was never long before we had to get out again and pull over another deadfall.

About six o'clock, we were thoroughly exhausted. Then we heard the first rumblings of thunder. I looked up and saw the sky had darkened and felt a cool breeze whiff over the water. *No way*, I thought. *This isn't happening.*

Fifteen minutes later, it was happening. And this wasn't just a little afternoon shower. One of the most violent storms I have ever experienced settled into our creek valley. Rain poured over us in heavy, pounding torrents. Thunder slammed and lighting whip-cracked the air a whitish blue with an intensity that I felt in my teeth. I was certain a tree beside me was going to explode in orange and yellow sparks at any moment. Albert got a bucket off the floor and put it over his head. I started to take it back from him to bail, then realized it was useless. The boat was filling up too fast. I got out and pulled it to shore, where I met the others.

We considered the facts. We had no food, no shelter, no flashlight, no cell reception, two terrified young boys, and no idea where we were.

Do we get out of the creek and stay the night or brave the storm and keep going?

We decided to keep going.

The boats were too heavy with water to motor so we had to pull them, wading chest-high in the now swollen creek. The rain was coming down so hard that we couldn't talk among ourselves, each of us waging our own little battle to persevere. Occasionally I asked Albert how he was doing and he told me from inside the bucket that he was fine.

Eventually, about sundown, the storm trailed off. The cicadas and frogs began to thrum in the still dusk. And just as it was getting too dark to see, we spotted the silhouette of the bridge through the trees ahead.

I suppose a man should be wary when trying to relive the days of his youth. Things aren't always as you remember them. Albert is thirteen now. Sometimes he finds a way to remind me that Majors Creek was the scariest time in his life. Maybe one day I'll come out and admit that, yes, it was pretty scary for me, too. For now, he's just got to believe that Dad is always in control.

CONVICTS

Before they were famous, we called them sheepshead. They were as useless as a channel cat. Trash fish. I vividly recall struggling to reel them in, convinced I had the biggest trout of the morning, only to see that black and white striped, bucktoothed idiot appear from the murky depths. And I'd grumble in my most disgusted tone, as I'd heard the older fisherman say, "Dang sheepshead."

A few years ago I had someone invite me to go fishing for "convicts." They said they were "tearing them up" on the rigs just outside the mouth of the bay. I'd never heard of a convict, but the enthusiasm and

117

urgency behind the invitation had me convinced that I'd better get in on catching whatever it was.

As it turned out, sometime since my youth, the sheepshead had been marketed into a sportfish carrying a nickname suggesting plenty of man points. We roared out into the Gulf in an expensive boat and cast live shrimp beside the rigs. As we pulled in one sheepshead after another, I had to keep glancing at my companions, suspicious I was the victim of a snipe hunt. But I soon realized they were serious about these things. Piling up man points.

"Do you eat them?" I asked.

"Filet them out, put them scale-down on the grill, and it's the best-tasting fish you'll ever eat," I was told.

There is someone somewhere that will tell you just about any fish, when cooked a certain way, is the best fish you'll ever eat. The only exception to this I know of is the channel cat. Which I suppose I'll write about one day. When I have absolutely nothing left to say about anything else.

Admittedly, I cleaned and cooked my convicts and they did taste good, at least as good as most other fish I've had.

A couple of years passed after my first sheepshead fishing trip. One morning this past summer, I took the kids after trout off Zundel's Wharf. Fishing with kids can be a tricky thing, especially something as hit-and-miss as trout fishing. One carries a nagging anxiety that if you don't catch something—anything—quick, you'll never get them out there again.

The bay was calm as a lake and the sun was starting to beat down on us. Our corks floated dead on the surface and the only noise was the steady humming of the bait aerator. For fifteen minutes, my kids had been lying in various contorted positions about the boat and I knew complaints were coming soon. I desperately needed to pull in some species of fish.

There were three more boats scattered nearby, no one catching anything. I imagined we were all relieved when the monotony was broken by a small beat-up skiff puttering up to the pilings. I recognized the driver as Blind Dog Mike, a friend from down the beach. Blind Dog didn't wave because he didn't see me. He can't see well at all. Which I suppose is how he got his name.

Blind Dog didn't anchor just outside the pilings like the rest of us, he drove right in among them. At first I suspected this was because he couldn't see, but I soon realized it was exactly what he had in mind. He clambered to the front of his skiff and tied the bow tight against a piling. Then he pulled a garden tool from the floor, something like an edger, and began scraping the piling below the water. I could hear the barnacles being raked and chipped away.

What the heck is he doing? I thought to myself.

But Blind Dog seemed to know exactly what he was doing, going about it all very systematically. And after a bit of scraping, he put the tool on the floor again, picked up a fishing rod, baited it with something I couldn't see, and dropped the line. In less than five seconds he was struggling against an enormous fish.

He hauled what must have been an eight-pound sheepshead into the boat. Then he did this two more times. Then he moved to another piling and did it three more times. After fishing a total of about ten minutes, he cranked his skiff and sputtered off, leaving the rest of us looking at each other. We were all within speaking distance, but each of us had been competitively silent and miserable for the past hour.

There was one boat that was closer to Blind Dog than the rest of us. We'd been so thoroughly shown up that I felt our competitive distance had been shattered. And I asked a question that one would never ask under different circumstances.

"What was he using for bait?"

"Looked like fiddler crabs," the man said.

The next weekend I woke the kids early and announced that we were going after "convicts." Just the name alone was enough to entice them into one more trip. I got a flathead shovel from the garden shed and met them at their little Stauter boat, which I assumed would be ideal for getting close to the pilings. Then we motored up the beach to a place where I'd seen plenty of fiddler crabs. At first we weren't sure they wouldn't pinch us and went about trying to catch them with bait nets. It wasn't long before we realized their pinchers weren't big enough to do anything more than scare us and we chased and grabbed them with our hands. And I'm thinking the kids are already having so much fun that the trip is a success no matter how many fish we end up catching.

With about a dozen fiddlers, we motored the rest of the way to Zundel's, pulled past that same scene of idle fishermen, and tied to one of the pilings. I proceeded to emulate Blind Dog's performance, scraping the piling with my shovel. Then the kids dropped their lines and it was on. They hauled in four monster convicts while the rest of the fisherman watched with that same defeated stare. And this time at a couple of twelve-year-olds. I couldn't have been prouder.

I'd redeemed myself with the kids, but I felt a bit guilty. The following week I called Blind Dog Mike to confess. Fortunately he was eager to share everything he knew about the process. He told me a few of his secret spots and all he knew about sheepshead. Like most tricks of the outdoorsman, he said it had been taught to him by an "old man." Scraping the piling chums the water with bits of barnacle, which attract the sheepshead. When the fish arrive, dangling before them is their favorite food, the fiddler crab. The sheepshead is territorial and you'll typically catch the biggest one first. And if you don't catch one within a few minutes, you need to move to another piling.

This sounded like dream fishing to me. A complete reversal of how it had always been. The biggest one first? And give up after a few minutes if you don't catch anything? Well, it works. And I'm getting lots of Dad points thanks to that old trash fish I once snubbed.

CONCLUSION

I LIVE IN MOBILE NOW, but Katie and I purchased Little Fish—the family cottage in Point Clear—from my siblings about fifteen years ago. I still spend my summers there, and my own family has learned to love the old home like I do. The place has changed, as places always do. I recently took a walk through Point Clear comparing what I see now to how it was when I was a boy.

Starting from Julep Point and moving south along Scenic 98, the tennis courts across the road from the Grand Hotel are gone. I recall as many as eight rubico courts, maybe more. That area was always low and prone to flooding and the courts were constantly underwater. I still love tennis and there was a time when I wanted to be really good at it and spent many hours practicing on those courts.

Barney and Cranky Pants, the two feared security guards, are gone. Even the giant pool is gone, replaced by a more modern version with a fake rock mountain and a poolside bar. This new pool is mostly for the guests, but the hotel, always considerate of the locals, built us our own on the other side of the golf course.

Most of the larger houses along the boardwalk have transitioned through remodeling and expansion and modernization. There are still a few of the old bay houses left, like Little Fish, but Point Clear is a year-round community now with a property owners association and even a Rotary Club.

Zundel's lane has always been there and it's always been public. We called it "the lane." And across from the lane is what used to be Luke's B&A Grocery. Never was sure what the B&A stood for. We used to walk up to Luke's and buy candy and Popsicles. He had a limited selection of groceries and bait and tackle. He also sold a lot of fuel to fill up the gas cans for our boats. But Point Clear has never supported a convenience store for long, or any retail operation for that matter. Luke's old building is used as an antique store now.

Just past Luke's (I'll always call it that) is the intersection of Scenic 98 and County Road 32. I suppose this would be called the business district of Point Clear. The post office used to be here before it moved up the road. Then the building was a bank and now is a real estate office. Across the street was a strip of connected business; the first used to be D-Mart, a metal building and convenience store that competed with Luke's for a short time. After Luke's closed, D-Mart hung on awhile longer, but it eventually closed as well. Connected to the D-Mart was the King Cole Club, a nightclub and sometimes a restaurant. Behind that was BooBoo's Paint and Body shop, where I had my first car painted. These building are gone. The only remaining piece of this original strip is the one at the end, though it looks abandoned.

If you stand at the intersection and look east, up County Road 32, the post office is about a quarter of a mile away. Just past it is the Point Clear Tennis Club, where I used to work. It's gone through several owners since Mrs. Arendall died. But one of my good friends I used to play tennis with, Matt McKelvain, never really left. He's the pro now and my daughter takes tennis lessons from him in the summertime.

Continuing south, toward Little Fish, not much has changed. You cross the Bailey's Creek Bridge, which has been rebuilt at least twice in my lifetime. Another mile and you come to an old abandoned building on the left. This used to be Nelson's, the stablest business I knew of in Point Clear. Like Luke, Pete Nelson sold gas, groceries, bait, tackle, and ice. It was like a real general store with most everything a person needed. Crab traps and cane poles hung from the ceiling. You could find a little hardware if you dug around. Most memorable was the walk-in ice cooler that sat outside the front door. He kept block ice inside. Walking in there on a sweltering summer day took a boy's breath away. It felt so good you just wanted to lie down in there.

That was pretty much my childhood orbit, and all of Point Clear. The Grand Hotel to Nelson's. I feel a bit like the place has moved on without me. Which it has. But I suppose everybody has a place and time in their life that stays fixed in their memory a certain way, regardless of how much it's really changed.